Wisdom of the Serpent

Wisdom of the Serpent

By James William Hornsby

Self-Published with assistance from
MIDNIGHT EXPRESS BOOKS

Wisdom of the Serpent

Self-Published with assistance from
MIDNIGHT EXPRESS BOOKS
POBox 69
Berryville AR 72616
MEBooks1@yahoo.com

Wisdom of the Serpent

By James William Hornsby

To Casey Jean; the girl in love with my talk about religion.
Thank you for all your help and support with getting this book published.
Your time and assistance played a crucial role in bringing it to fruition. You
helped to make my dream come true. The time you took from your own life,
to be a part of mine, is priceless and I pray that I never let you forget it.
Thank you. I love you.

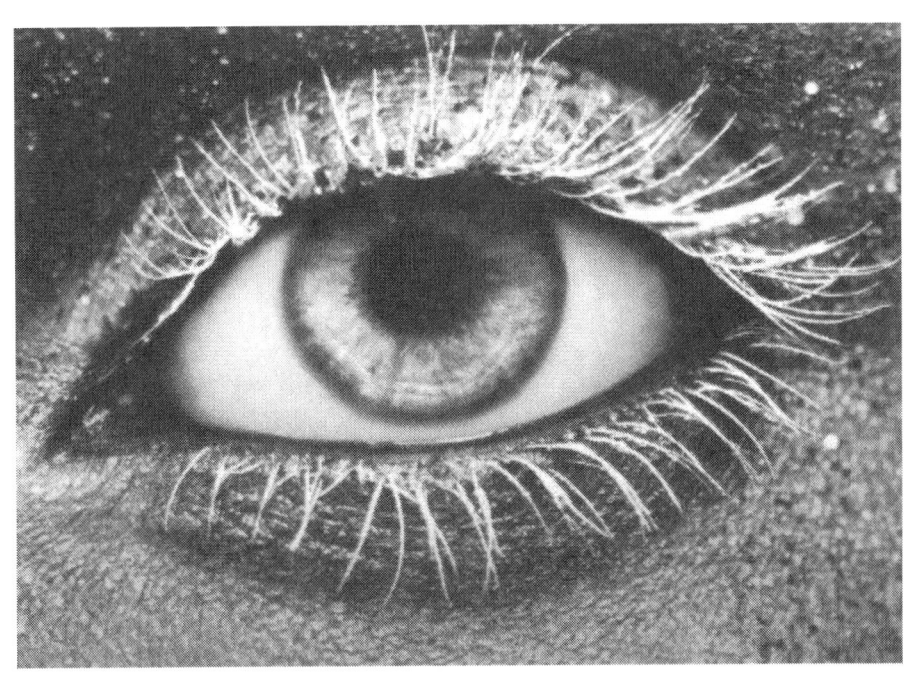

322

IT IS BETTER TO BE ALIVE-DEAD
THAN TO BE OF THOSE WHO ARE DEAD-ALIVE

Table of Contents

A LOST KEY

"There's not the smallest orb which thou beholds't
But in his motion like an angel sings,
Still quiring to the young eye'd cherubins;
Such harmony is in immortal souls;
But whilst this muddy vesture of decay
Doth grossly close it in, we cannot hear it. "

-The Merchant of Venice, IV, 1

"To slip the 'muddy vesture of decay', in which the essence of our immortal soul like a sleeping princess lies entombed, is the Great Work. It is the sacred quest of the mystic, alchemist, yogi and magician, but it is also the inescapable destiny of every unit of evolving consciousness in the universe.

But how can we go about extricating this pristine essence from the tomb that so "grossly" closes us in? Can we chip it away like a cocoon? Can we shed it like a serpent's skin? Can we wash ourselves clean of it?

We can try. Indeed, plotting the escape from this prison of matter is the *'raison-detre'* of the world's great religions. As Hindus and Buddhists, [They] deny it as illusion; as Christians, [They] attempt to bribe [Their] way free with a ransomed savior and, together with the other 'people of the Book'-*Muslims and Jews*-[They] hate it and fear it as a devil, make war upon it as an enemy, flee from it as sin, and (discarding God-given common sense) gamble [Their] souls on the historicity of myths and obedience to scriptural law so that, after death, [They] might discover [They] have won the prize of immortality.

Such efforts in and of themselves will remain forever doomed for, while they are effective instruments for spiritual crowd control, they ignore one very fundamental and paradoxical cosmic truth. That is, the tomb of matter, the "muddy vesture of decay", is itself an inextricable part of the essence of our immortal soul. For is it not written that the temple of initiation is also a tomb?

[O]ne can focus intensely upon the mystery teachings of the past without isolating oneself from the discoveries and revelations of the present; that [O]ne can unite the modern sciences of the mind with the wonder and wisdom of the ages.

[In] the twilight of the golden ages of Egypt and Greece [a number of individuals] shared their wisdom in a body of mystical texts supposedly written by the God Thoth, or Hermes, or Hermes Trismegistos. Foremost among these is one that bears the name of its mythical author, *The Emerald Tablets of Hermes.*

It is true and no lie, certain, and to be de-

1

*pended upon, that the superior agrees with
the inferior, and the inferior with superior,
to effect that one truly wonderful work.*

-Manly P. Hall
Lost Keys of Freemasonry
(Richmond, VA; Macoy 1968)
p. 96

Verses five and six go on to provide the diligent aspirant the mystic key by which he or she can arise from the tomb of matter even while acknowledging that the tomb is an integral part of the self.

*The power is perfect, after it has been united
with a spirituous Earth. Separate the spirituous Earth from the dense or crude Earth by
means of a gentle heat, with much attention.*
-Manly P. Hall
Lost Keys, p.96

It is the profoundest of cosmic ironies. The divine power, our true spiritual essence, does not achieve perfection until it hits the rock bottom of the cosmos -the dense crude earth. It remains imperfect until the moment of entombment for the simple reason that, until the dark nadir is reached, the experiential adventure of existence remains incomplete and self is not yet endowed with the entire spectrum of light of consciousness—from spirit to matter, from the highest high to the lowest low.

This is why Hermetic tradition informs us that the highest angelic hosts envy the children of the dust because humans have something they will never have -a little bit of everything from top to bottom. High as they are, the angels are stuck in divine middle management without a complete stash of the raw material necessary to clone themselves to perfect godhead. Aleister Crowely describes this process as "...the general doctrine that the climax of the Descent [I]nto Matter is the signal for the redintegration[1] by spirit." Once the lowest low has been reached, the power is perfect and the process of return is initiated.

The Emerald Tablets of Hermes tells us how to begin. We are to "separate the spirituous earth from the dense or crude earth, by means of a gentle heat, with much attention." This doesn't mean we are to cook ourselves over a low flame (although in the symbolic language of alchemy, that's pretty much what we do). It means that through a slow, balanced, and gentle process we are (with great attention) to distill the essence of our being, the song

---

[1] An archaic word meaning 'restoration to a former state'

2

of our soul, from the muddy vesture of decay.

This is the initiatory process of the Hermetics old and new—a balanced and gentle program of study, practice, and meditation mixed with the effects of one's own inherited destiny (whether you call that luck, good fortune, or karma).

Initiation is not a reward for achievement or a seal of attainment. Indeed, the initiate may never attain (at least not in this incarnation). Initiation means to "begin", and the first question the candidate is asked at the threshold of the Temple is simply, "Are you ready to begin?"

-Lon Milo DuQuette
The New Hermetics
Foreword, XV

"Are you ready to begin?"

CHAPTER ONE

KNOW THYSELF

There will be many persons setting out to read the instant book who have no idea or clue as to his or her true position within the basic groups, or subgroups, of society. It is the author's intention to draw a radical and metaphorical *line in the sand* in order that, by the end of this book or even this very chapter, the reader will have placed his or her own self into one of the categories listed hereafter.

Have you ever started reading a book and after you have already begun you realize that the way in which the author has employed various words or phrases is not the same as the way they would be commonly used in an average conversation? Perhaps you have read the book entitled *A Clockwork Orange*, which itself is considered to be a literary masterpiece, and you very quickly realized that the language, as used in that particular book, might mean something radically different than the meaning it has in our current English. The author's ability there to teach the reader a whole new language, or slang, as the reader progresses through the book is what some critics believe puts *A Clockwork Orange* into the category of a masterpiece. In general, the author here agrees.

In the text at hand, the author does not intend to place himself among the ranks of the masterpieces, nor is it his intention to teach the reader a language or slang as he or she progresses through this body of work. The author here does, however, use common terms, words, and/or phrases in a manner that is not currently employed by the average person you may meet on the street.

Well, what better time would there be to familiarize the reader with these terms, or at least the ones most commonly employed, than in the beginning of the document? Only makes sense right?

For these reasons, the author here asks that you please bear with him as he provides you, the reader, with the definition he attributes to some simple terms or words whose definition is most likely different than the definition a person would normally be familiar with or able to recognize. Hang in there, this text is worth reading to those in possession of the ability to see beyond the surface and recognize the 'big picture'.

Group One: The Gods and Goddesses

Many apply recognition, conception, and definition of divinity to the word(s) God and Goddess. Some people use the term in a monotheistic way to describe their belief in a single and principal object of faith and worship, whereas some employ the very same term in a pluralistic way to describe their belief in a pantheon, or at least dual, object of faith and worship. The latter group use the term Goddess equally with the term God in order to describe the feminine aspect(s), or persona(s), of such a pantheon. The former will almost never use the term Goddess except where their particular belief allows for a God that can be both masculine and feminine or at least portray both of those aspects within the same form. Interestingly, and perhaps a bit suspiciously, almost all forms of monotheistic beliefs depict deity in masculine form; that is, GOD as a He. Either way, the terms are most often put to use to refer to supernatural, divine, or mythical beings who either:

A. Created the known universe including Earth and its' inhabitants; or

B. rule over Earth or the material plane, including the universe, and control its forces and energies by way of their own omnipotence or higher status in evolution, such as that gained through reincarnation and sometimes simply by 'right'.

The author briefly notes, without any personal opinion of its validity, that there do exist certain theosophical and philosophical movements, such as, but not limited to, the Islamic 'Five-Percenters', who often refer to themselves as *gods* upon reaching or attaining a certain status or degree within their system of teaching a curriculum considered to be secret knowledge. Further, along this same line of thought, the author would remind the reader that the Christian character Jesus, considered to be a Master in the Judeao-Christian path, specifically asked his disciples, as recorded in the Gospel of John, "Know Ye not that Ye are Gods?"

The author here beseeches the reader to consider, at least for the duration of this book, that there exists another way to use the terms noted above other than the ways previously described.

Let us open our minds, broaden our horizons, and consider the term God and Goddess as a means of describing or referring to a higher, more developed, and more intelligent race of beings. Today, in the twenty-first century, we would commonly label these beings as 'aliens'; however, the author chooses to shy from employing the word alien due to the fact that it will usually evoke mental pictures of little green men with huge heads and large almond shaped eyes. Instead, the author asks that you consider a being with the same basic bodily form as earthly humanity; although, it would be normal to find variations in the details just as variations naturally exist in humanity and any other species or class/sub-class of life-forms. Consider this being, or person, as one who possesses seemingly otherworldly powers of mind and body that you as yet do not possess, such as a sophistication of machinery and technology unknown to humans at present, and intelligence that humanity has simply not aspired to yet. Perhaps they are simply in possession of the ability to utilize their brain or mind one hundred percent and now have complete and total control of their bodies, including their voluntary and involuntary nervous systems. Perhaps they are able to think and use the collective wisdom or knowledge of a group-mind. Perhaps they have evolved their Light-Bodies (astral-body/subtle-body/ka) to the point where they are no longer bound by the confines and restrictions of the dense Material-Body (physical-body) and are able to exist at a much higher frequency than the life forms indigenous to Earth.

If such a person were to stand before you, is it not reasonable that he or she might seem to be a God or Goddess if one would apply the characteristics of the common concept of Gods, Angels, Spirits, etc.? With that in mind, think of humanity as it existed two thousand years ago when the Jewish religion was first beginning to give way to the Christian rite. Think of mankind seven thousand; ten thousand; or twenty thousand years ago. Is it not easy to fathom how the term God first originated and was then distinctly used to refer to one, any, or all of the supernatural beings with their supernatural capabilities that presented themselves so readily and openly to early mankind?

At this point in time, in the beginning of the New Age, only certain, chosen people will hear the words of the Gods and only certain, chosen people will be part of the revelations to come. The chosen are Illuminati.

The image of this race of beings, as described above, might call to mind an average human, though admittedly the human would lack the capabilities of that beings race. Here, the author asks that the reader consider the following quote in light of the fore-going considerations: "And God proceeded to create the man in His image, in God's image He created them; the male and the female, He created them." Genesis, 1:27.

Plato, in *The Banquet*, while mentioning the Gods, on every page for the entirety of his discourse, indicates that by the term Gods he means a class of beings far lower in the scale than the Primary or Secondary Deities, or even those in charge over the creation of matter, and but one grade higher than men.

Likewise, in the text you are reading, and for the duration thereof, the author asks that the reader conceptualize, or refer to, this higher race of beings (who took it upon themselves to populate planet Earth with the life we know today as humanity) any time that the term God or Goddess might be employed.

Group Two: Illuminati and Enlightened Ones

What was your first reaction at reading the word Illuminati? Believe it or not, but your initial internal reaction to that single word is of utmost importance to the determination of who and what you are, as an incarnate being, and at what place you currently find yourself in your personal and universal evolution. Please mark and highlight the internal feeling that you experienced when you first read the above word and do your best to remember this feeling when you are asked to do so at the end of this chapter. This word, Illuminati, is a Latin word which basically translates to mean Enlightened One(s). Perhaps you already consider yourself to be an Enlightened One?

With that thought in mind, consider how many millions have heard the word Illuminati and trembled from fear, raised their fists in anger or simply scoffed at the idea that there might be those amongst their peers (humanity) who have reached or aspired to an elevated echelon of knowledge, wisdom, understanding and evolution of the Light-Body? Or, perhaps those Illuminati have simply amassed a grander economic status than the average person and this fact places them in positions where they are able to instill their own beliefs or will onto and into society. Now consider where the feelings of fear, anger, envy and disbelief stem from within the average human being.

The author sets forth that it is usually one's own realization of a certain self-lack that causes these reactions to the word. When one realizes that one is less important, less advanced, less wealthy, less intelligent, or less evolved than the next being it is one thing, and one might take steps to improve their own personal position; however, when you admit that your status has been determined by the works, or lack thereof, of your very own hands and choices, most cannot simply accept this as the truth and do something to create a change. Rather, they put up a wall, a front, and lash out against the beauty; but really, who has kept them from this beauty? Philosophically speaking, they have kept themselves from it by refusing to see it and take the steps necessary to obtain it.

Strategically speaking, it has been Illuminati who have ensured that only the worthy receive it, which consists only of those who took measures in a previous era to build the Temple. This process has taken form as the proverbial veil of rhetoric used to conceal the Truth in Light while simultaneously causing that Light to be considered darkness by the biggest portion of the uninformed and un-enlightened human population.

Many are used to applying the term Illuminati to a 'mystical elite' of wealthy individuals who hoard the earth's resources for themselves and who secretly plot, behind the scenes, to control world governments and enslave the masses of humanity in order that those of the elite would have a more leisurely, enjoyable, desirable and luxurious way of life. As you will see in the coming chapters, the author accepts this definition, though not in the negative light in which it is usually viewed.

Also true is that in recent history there did exist a secret-society, or brotherhood, known as the Order of Illuminati in Bavaria, Hungary. Two well distinguished gentlemen who claimed title as Illuminati were none other than the illustrious Adam Weishaupt and General Albert Pike, who himself was also the 33° Sovereign Grand Commander of Scottish-Rite Masonry, Southern Jurisdiction, A.F. & A.M. Their memoirs and correspondences are on record for the reader who is ever curious and who desires to study in order to show themselves approved. The author here does not necessarily condone or agree with any of the 'personal' opinions or beliefs held by these two well-known gentlemen concerning race, ethnicity, nationality, sex, sexuality, etc. The author well understands how it is possible for enlightened men and women to still be limited by the views or prejudices popular to their particular era, even when such views, in a later era, are considered to be held only by those of the ignorant type; in short, sometimes we are all swayed by the collective mind of the human race even though it is our explicit goal to transcend the same.

It is not readily known if the order still exists to this day; however, on record it is noted to be dissolved and no longer functioning. There is rumor however that the door to the Order of Illuminati is secretly guarded by many names and occupational titles that are still in existence today. Entry through that portal is what the author truly seeks by way of the instant instrument. May this text be a beacon and radar; the author prays to be approached. However, as this text is not an attempted expose of the Order of Illuminati, let us continue.

What is it then that those certain and specific individuals are knowledgeable of that others are not? What are the Enlightened Ones aware of that the overwhelming majority of humanity is not?

In this book, the Enlightened Ones are defined as those individuals who know that humanity was created by an extra-terrestrial and extra-dimensional race that used their very own DNA as a basis for their creation(s) and who thereby made humanity in their own image. Further, the Enlightened Ones are not simply aware of this knowledge, but are in active and conscious pursuit of:

- Activating this portion of themselves and their DNA;
- Reaching out to the Gods; and
- The evolution of the Enlightened Ones by and through the express teachings of, and literal encounters with, the Gods themselves.

Still further, the Enlightened Ones are aware of, and accept wholeheartedly, that most of humanity will not reach the state of enlightenment to which Illuminati have attained. The Enlightened Ones have accepted the fact that only those who choose the Path of Enlightenment, and stay on it, deserve to know. The Enlightened Ones know that the true nature of the universe, as well as life, exists simultaneously with, and lay hidden behind, what most would commonly consider to be 'reality'. They know that Nature and everything within it are merely illusions alluding to the true realities of infinity and divinity. The Enlightened Ones are not only aware of and accepting of the widespread programming taking place in world-society which is used to conceal Truth from the Masses, but are also actively promoting it at every level of social interaction thereby uniformly ensuring that the majority of the Masses choose to keep themselves in 'darkness'.

Illuminati know that We are the living-gods of creation who are really being worshipped through orthodox religion.

The Enlightened Ones' grand view is not to be shunned. It is a natural, as well as empirical, view that is correct in every facet. All have access to the Truth, yet so very few are spiritually evolved enough to see the Truth even when it is so lightly veiled. Most would rather believe in the fairy-tale or live by faith alone because the Path of Enlightenment offers hard work, in the building of the Temple, where the paths of dogmatic religion offer ease and convenience. When attempting to understand the basic mindset of the Enlightened Ones, which is basically 'us-against-them', one should carefully consider the following words:

> "The problem with any philosophical consideration is that once you open a door in your mind, you can never close it. Once you learn something, you can never convince your mind that you didn't learn it. If you learn the world is round, you can never fit in with a world that thinks it's flat. "

> -Ted Dekker
> *The Priests Graveyard*

Group Three: The Masses

This is the easiest term for the author to define because it means almost exactly the same thing as used in this text as it would in its normal and everyday use. The Masses are the majority of humanity, roughly eighty-five percent of Earth's population, who either:

A. Arrogantly believe or assume that any intelligent life higher than that of the human race does not and cannot exist;

B. Cannot transcend the brain-washing, social-conditioning and instilled ideals that they have been constantly subjected to since birth;

C. Are content, happy, or complaisant with what they perceive to be reality along with their station or role in it;

D. Are those who have discovered or been made aware of the Truth and its' higher realities but have made a conscious and informed decision to continue in their prior footsteps, pretending to block out what has been shown or given to them or re-submitting to the social brainwashing they were previously immersed in; or,

E. Follow and support the Illuminati agenda and/or are practitioners of The Craft in one form or another.

The Masses mostly have no clue or idea as to their alien origin, the secrets existing dormant within themselves, or the truth in regards to their make-believe 'GODS' and religions. The Masses are not aware of the individuals amongst them who consider Them to be merely animals because of the fact that they fail to awaken the god-material existing within themselves.

The Masses are not aware of those amongst them who keep from them the very secrets that would allow them to rise up from the dust and ascend to the stars. The Masses are mostly ignorant to the fact that the Enlightened Ones or the Gods (as defined herein) even exist.

The Masses are mostly ignorant of the fact that they are subjected to wide scale programming (conditioning) on a daily basis or that it is designed with the intended purpose of keeping them from becoming aware of the Truth and keeping them in darkness in an effort to ensure that only those who possess strength of mind, strength of will, knowledge of true consciousness and evolution of the Light-Body are awakened out of the matrix of humanity and materialism; those who become aware, become de-sensitized by the constant bombardment of their psyche with social propaganda to the point where they cease to remain conscious of it. A screening process if you will. The Masses, so long as they remain in their darkened state, are viewed by both the Gods and Enlightened Ones as mere chattel.

The author will now expound on the basic condition of each sub-group of the Masses, listed as A thru E above, in order to provide a more clear insight of whom, why and how they have been placed into the group entitled the Masses.

Sub-Group A

These individuals buy into the belief that intelligent life exists no place other than Earth, except sometimes maybe in 'heaven', and believe that the current state of earthly sophistication and technology now possessed by mankind is at its highest point in history or any other time and place or by any other people(s) who might have existed in ancient civilizations. They seek to magnify any alleged mistakes made by ancient societies, or discrepancies in anatomy, physiology or other modern sciences to an inordinate extent so as to gratify their self-love and gain the idea of their own superiority of learning until the intellectual splendor which adorns the ages of the past is wholly lost upon them.

These individuals tend to forget that merely five-hundred years ago our current state of humanity lacked the ability to read and write except for the privileged few who were priests or other administrators of the Church. Three hundred years ago man could not harness the energies of Nature such as electricity, atom fusion/fission, etc. These individuals also overlook, either purposely or ignorantly, the multitude of ancient writings or drawings depicting a higher level of insight into the forces of nature as well as technology, such as the ancient Mayan's or Egyptian's depictions of flying craft (vehicles) using what appears to be crystals or stones as their sources of energy.

Individuals in Sub-Group A tend to harbor their belief in the superiority of humankind out of pride. It is an egotistical attempt to place themselves personally (along with the rest of humanity) at the apex of either creation or life. Sometimes these individuals are afraid to consider that life higher than that of humanity might exist because that consideration would lead them to consider just how weak humanity may be when compared to other and higher forms of evolved life. Some individuals within this sub-group harbor this belief simply because they have been told to do so by others whom they view as superior to themselves such as parents, scientists, teachers, theologians, religious leaders, etc. Many times, their inward sense of insecurity leads them to insist otherwise outwardly, but such is normally a vain attempt to convince others, as well as themselves, that their insecurity does not exist and that their beliefs are theirs even though they simply repeat the dogma of their prescribed religion. Usually almost no belief or thought surrounding that particular belief system is truly their own.

Sub-Group B

The individuals in this sub-group have mostly been 'swept away' by the worlds many religions and the feelings or emotions their religious leaders have been able to call forth from them during religious worship gatherings. These individuals have been totally blinded, to the point of automatism, by the interpretations of the ancient manuscripts, as set forth by their religious leaders. These interpretations usually consist of an outline of humanities creation and mankind's past relationship and interaction with the extra-terrestrial or extra-dimensional race of beings who created Them which the religious leaders interpret as 'GOD'.

These individuals will not let go of the notions set forth by their religious teachers, parents, and the many books they have turned to in order to receive instruction from other men concerning how they should worship deity; nor would they choose to let go, even if that choice was an option for them. Sadly it is not. These people cannot make this choice, or even consider it for that matter, because the indoctrination and brainwashing they have been subjected to (and willingly continue to be subjected to) is total and complete.

First, their beliefs were put into place by their parents who, in a similar manner, were already in the final stages of conditioning themselves. Later, religious leaders, spouses, friends, humanity in general and yes, even the social programming advanced upon them by the Enlightened Ones, have served to solidify and perpetuate their belief in the lie. No matter how you present an argument which falls contrary to their individual religious belief system, or how much sense you make to these people, they are simply incapable of relinquishing their conditioned religious responses or using the reasoning that is taught in the very religious books they claim to believe in even though these very same stories are relied upon by them (although in a diluted and manipulated form) to uphold their ideas or religion. This is not to say, expressly, that their books contain inaccurate information or no truth whatsoever but more to say that it is presented to, and then used by, them in a convoluted manner as a direct result of manipulation, deceit and conditioning. To get them to see anything other than that which their particular faith dictates will not happen because it is actually not possible for these particular individuals.

The part of these individuals mind and DNA that ever could have realized the Truth has been effectively 'locked' and they are incapable of 'unlocking' it to gain access to personal insights or anything other than their accepted dogmas and doctrines. Even when these people are in agreement with a particular point being presented to them, they will always revert back to their programming because they have always failed to think and reason for themselves until it became too late and their programming was complete. Now, it has a life of its own and is beyond their control. Just as in their allegory of Moses and Egypt's Pharaoh, their hearts have been hardened and they are incapable of receiving Light.

Though these peoples condition is mostly attributable to others rather than themselves, their very dogma will ultimately be their demise. It will control their decision between foregoing their intolerable disease (religious indoctrination) and becoming a member of the New Age or submitting to extinction. These individuals suffer from the psychosis best described as 'fear-overrides-reason' and because of that fear they can never circumscribe their desires nor place their passions within due bounds. Their fear of The End, as outlined in their religious books, will cause them to live out the very role they have been conditioned to play in the 'end times'. Their fear of the New Age will cause them to be victims of the same.

Sub-Group C

The individuals considered in this sub-group shy away from anything in life that requires effort or confrontation. Any matters or ideals that might cause them discomfort or variance from what they consider to be the easy or good life will not be considered or acknowledged by these persons. These individuals are mostly amiable and are willingly compliant with any laws or changes in law, as well as in other matters where family, friends, religious leaders, political leaders, governments, role-models, etc. tell them what they should be or how they should act. These people make up the 'average-Joe' who goes to work, gets paid, goes home, spends their money and then repeats the cycle, always returning what was temporarily allotted to them (monetary credits), even if not right away, such as in cases where one might invest or plan for retirement. These people are content with their clothes, cars, homes, boats, motorcycles, phones, etc. and actually believe they own those things and that the possessions are actually theirs; however, let them fail to pay their taxes and see if Uncle Sam recognizes their ownership or if He is able to confiscate their luxuries and amenities from them at will. In short, they are happy with what they have at the present and indeed might possess quite a bit of material wealth, some even having the intention of becoming wealthier. These individuals will remain this way so long as they are allowed to pursue 'the good life' as they believe it to be. In truth, they are socio-economic slaves, ever returning the credits their masters bestow upon them in order to experience happiness from the use of the items they collect with their so-called 'money'.

These individuals do not sincerely consider stepping 'outside-the-box' and have mostly accepted their lot, or position, in life and society. They loathe being the one who might cause 'ripples in the pond'. They are content with providing service to the Enlightened Ones and the Gods, although they are mostly never aware that this is the very reason that the socio-economic system of neo-slavery was introduced. It gave the slaves a sense of owning part of the master's wealth and it gave the slave the illusive freedom to choose what station of slavery he would submit to and what sense of enjoyment he would obtain from said station such as wealth, free-time, pursuit of happiness, family life, possession of material objects, etc. In this socioeconomic system of slavery the chains are not literal chains placed onto the slave from the outside; rather, the chains are internally chosen by the slaves themselves and the bindings are placed upon the subtle-bodies (i.e., the Light-Body, Thought-Body, Desire-Body, etc.). As such, the socioeconomic slave does not even realize he or she has the ability to be master because much of their entire life has been spent in service to the individual master of his or her own choosing while he/she personally assumed identity as the slave. Further, this form of slavery does not readily and openly discriminate amongst the many different shades of skin tone; thus, again, the slavery lay hidden beneath the surface in contrast with the slavery of ancient times when slavery was skin-deep and mostly depended upon the individual's skin color, race, nationality or tribal origin. Neither are these individuals aware that they help to make up a majority of the chattel of their governments and rulers which is depended upon by those governments and rulers to further the global economic system and to interact with one another in a global banking mechanism used by the world's elite.

These individuals can be compared to the shifting sands of the desert or the winding and flowing schools of fish in the ocean. Point them in one direction today and they will gladly steer themselves that way, believing entirely that it is best to 'go with the flow' and that it is really their choice that they are doing so. Tomorrow, point the same ones in the total opposite direction and again they will be happy to comply and proceed with their everyday mundane life so long as they possess a mediocre level of contentment, happiness, luxury and toys with which to focus their attention and immerse themselves in. New cell-phone anybody!?

These individuals, though seeing, cannot see; though hearing, they cannot hear.

Sub-Group D

The individuals in this sub-group might be the most detested, and damned, of all of the Masses because they are the ones who have had opportunity, and possess the mental and spiritual capacity, to rise from the category in which they currently reside (the Masses) and obtain true enlightenment.

However, after full and intelligent consideration of Truth, these individuals choose to remain in the darkness in which they have lived their entire lives.

These individuals usually turn away from the Truth because once knowing Truth, it takes an internal effort to apply it in everyday life in order to properly build the Temple. It takes effort to receive enlightenment as well as many decisions and/or acts which defy or contradict our society's current understanding of right or wrong, ethics, values and rules of engagement. In some circumstances, these individuals are blatantly and freely given jewels of faith and truth in a manner not normally allowed or practiced and are also provided the explicit tools and exercises required to build the Temple of Light; however, these individuals will often still want more. What they have not the courage to say to those who are already in possession of the knowledge of Self is that they want to know, want you to teach it to them freely and simply as if you were teaching them to bake brownies, and then they would like you to do it for them also, or magically bestow upon them the attributes, gifts and powers attained during the stages of enlightenment.

They realize that they have been given a full slice of the proverbial pie and they did not have to put in work, or pay, to gain it. Because they obtained it freely and without personal sacrifice or effort, such as intense study or practice, they cannot appreciate that which they were given and therefore they also do not want to put forth the effort it takes to eat it; they want YOU to eat it for them. These individuals represent those of the 'Knowers' who were never required to first be 'Thinkers' and as such, they will most always fail to ever become 'Doers'. Thus, they will fail to gain enlightenment and will fall to the side of The Path in the same manner that the chaff falls to the wayside of the trade route.

Many times the individual in this sub-group will use the small portion of knowledge or truth that was given to him or her in a manner, or as a tool, to manipulate others also of the Masses, or bend them to their will. They do not view what has been given to them as precious and so use it in any manner they like with reckless disregard of any repercussions of their actions.

These individuals can be dangerous to the Enlightened Ones and are mostly wanting of destruction, as they have no place in the system of the New Age; not even a place amongst the Masses or chattel.

Sub-Group E

The individuals who make up this subgroup are the believers in the Synarchy of Illuminati and are the citizens of the Reptilian Empire. This group consists of the followers, believers, and devotees of the Enlightened Ones. Most often, but not always, these individuals are approximately forty-five years of age or younger. They make up what can be viewed as the newer or younger generations whose consciousness and awareness is, on average, more naturally evolved than the older generations; however, it should be noted that there will naturally be some people from the older generations who will find that they are a part of this subgroup also.

Individuals in this group have found it unreasonable to believe and blindly follow the leaders and traditions of orthodox religions as well as the brainwashing doctrines promoted by those same religions. Many of these persons will already be enchanted followers or practitioners of The Craft in one form or another. As such, they are already treading the Path of Enlightenment and are believers in one or more of the many Luciferian Doctrines of Light.

These are the persons who find themselves fascinated and engrossed with the thoughts, ideas and practice of ritual magic and the so-called pagan doctrines. They are the ones who spend time on the internet reviewing and learning about subjects such as, but not limited to, Illuminati, witchcraft, magic, secret-societies, Egypt, U.F.O.'s, secret governments, aliens, the New World Order and other subjects such as these which are equally relative to the Synarchy of the Reptilian Empire. When unable to access the internet, these persons will find and review these same subjects in books and/or visit social-arenas where they can discuss this type of criteria with other like-minded individuals.

This group consists of those who not only believe in Illuminati, but will elect to become citizens of the Reptilian Empire, the One World Order, under rule of the Enlightened Ones and the extra-terrestrial and inter-dimensional Gods and Goddesses mentioned previously. Further, these citizens will openly promote the cause of the Enlightened Ones in order to bring as many individuals, previously mentioned in subgroups A thru D, to the Light as is possible.

These persons either already consider themselves to be Illuminati, but do not know who to turn to with that revelation, or desire to reach that status and be one of Us; further, these individuals are ready and willing to take any and all necessary measures to be numbered and counted as Illuminati.

Those of this subgroup live by the Light of the Serpent and are of one mind and accord with Illuminati. They will be the trusted caretakers, friends and colleagues of those who will rule The Empire. They will enjoy luxuries heretofore unheard of and unthought-of in exchange for their undying and complete loyalty to the Order of the Empire.

Remember, when considering the fear and resentment most of the Masses bestow upon Illuminati, Enlightened Ones should ever remember:

"DAMNANT QUOD NON INTELLIGUNT"

More Clarification

First and foremost, the race of beings that the author has defined as the Gods and Goddesses will be referred to as such, in order to differentiate them from humans, even Illuminati.

Next, the reader should pay close attention to the terms 'We/They',

'Us/Them', 'Our/Their' and to how these specific pronouns are used by the author. The reader should understand that when the term 'We' is used, the author is referring to those individuals who consist of, or make up, the afore-noted Enlightened Ones, although membership in a certain 'Order' or 'Se-cret-Society' is not required for a person to fall into this category. All that is required is that the individual be in true possession of the consciousness of 'Self', working to evolve the Light-Body and to be of a mindset described previously; further, a person who is truly enlightened will not fail to see the purpose of and need for the age-old 'agenda' that is currently bringing the New Age into fruition. To immediately put the term into an understandable use, the author sets forth the following example statement: "We are Illumina-ti. We know that We alone deserve to partake of the Tree of Life also. Know-ing this, We lay claim to Our birthright under the Master of Light. Let Us live Our lives in true enlightenment under Our true benefactor and let Us re-ject the One who desired to keep Us in darkness. It is Our destiny to be like the Most High and to rule creation as We evolve. It is Our destiny, as Chil-dren of Light, to walk into the Sun, thereby re-entering the Garden of Eden."

When the author uses the term 'They', the reader should understand that he is referring to those who are part of the group referred to as the Masses. The same applies to the term 'Them'. To now put these terms into immediate and understandable use, the author again employs an example statement: "Unbeknownst to Them, They are the secret enemy and have been for ages. Let Us rule over the ignorant followers of the Oppressor and use Their blind-ness against Them for Our benefit lest They seek to drag Us back into the darkness from which We have evolved. In failing to see what is before Their very eyes, They have shown Themselves to be unworthy of Light. We must act now and must not miss Our opportunity."

Self-Awareness

By now the reader may have begun to realize something about his or her-self that they were not aware of previous to reading this entire chapter. This first chapter was unknowingly the place and time in which the 'two sides', and the fine line between them, was made perfectly clear.

Christianity's Jesus did not come to bring unity to humanity; rather, He clearly stated that He came to bring division and that His way would cause enmity between mother and daughter, father and son, and so forth.

Let this chapter be the line which divides Illuminati from those of the dark.

Most readers will have already realized, figured or decided which group, and possibly sub-group, he or she truly belongs to. Some will be in denial and not wish to admit the group they really belong to because they have been shown a truth about themselves that lay hidden up until the point of this small self-realization. To be in denial of which group one belongs to is noth-ing more than the choice of self-delusion and one would only be fooling one's own self. If you are unhappy with the category you have determined yourself to be part of, then the time to begin the journey of Self-Evolution is at hand; that is, if you can find the courage.

For those who have already released their identification with the Ego to exist in Light, congratulations. You will find the remainder of this text intriguing and will no doubt understand how and why the author has attempted this text.

The New Age must be brought into fruition using Their understanding, interpretations, and expectations of the age-old plans set forth within Their very own holy books.

Those in darkness will scoff at the author's audacity; however, those with eyes to see and ears to hear will gain further insight into the underlying elements of our current society and the fears set forth by religion that currently drives society and is preventing the full evolution into the New Age. You will also gain further insight into the entitlement which is now so closely within Our grasp.

The author would gladly guide the Masses onto the war-plain of Illuminati and is fully capable of evoking Their personal decision to go forth thereon of Their own free-will and accord. Consider this prophecy: "The Age of Self is at hand."

We must now OPENLY bring it forth and remove the veil that has kept Our agenda from the eyes of those who would oppose Her Light.

In considering Our treatment and stance concerning those of the Masses who would not choose enlightenment over the darkness in which They currently reside, We must remember the words of the Sun: "Cast not Thy pearl before swine, lest They turn and rend Thee with it." For this very reason, They have been deceived until the appointed time. That time is at hand and now let Them receive Truth in order that They may decide.

Here, the author asks the reader to remember his or her initial reaction to the word Illuminati. Are you able to understand now, after reading the division creating criteria provided afore, the reason the author had you highlight that reaction? If not, here is why.

The initial reaction to that word BEFORE you read the entire chapter was the true reaction indicative of your status; any reaction you might have had after reading the entire chapter may have been the brain or intellects' way of pridefully hiding Truth from the 'I'.

CHAPTER TWO

AN ALTERNATE PERCEPTION

LET THOSE RULED BY PASSION FLEE THIS PLACE; LET THOSE WHO REASON, ENTER.

In order to truly be able to consider yourself enlightened, an individual must be in a state of complete freedom of thought and cognizance; that is, you must have reached a point where the conditioning that you have been subjected to throughout your life no longer supersedes thinking, reasoning, or cognizant deduction. You must be in possession of the ability to see for yourself, which means being able to consider any one subject, no matter how different or unpopular, without having a conditioned, pre-determined or predisposed idea or view which you would unconsciously use to base your thinking and consideration and with which you would also unconsciously use to conceal from yourself the Light which you might otherwise use to gain a greater understanding of that subject.

The author does not expect every reader to hold the explicit or exact beliefs in which he does, but would expect any fellow considering himself or herself to be enlightened to be able to first acknowledge that the particular beliefs held by the author concerning deity is correct simply because they are 'correct' for the author. Secondly, such a fellow would be expected to be able to objectively consider the author's beliefs and opinions; finding the common theme(s) existing in any differing belief systems. Finally, such a fellow should be able to accept that all beliefs, even those of the 'Abrahamic-Religions' when they are considered in the manner in which they were meant, exist together in complete unity and are collectively considered to be the whole of the Luciferian Doctrine (doctrines which promote enlightenment of mankind).

The author would suggest that humanity, namely the Masses, currently have in Their possession some truth as contained within Their holy books such as the Torah, Holy Bible and Quran. However, the Truth has been manipulated therein by man's efforts to create organized religion, which garners power, fame, and fortune. The manipulation has reached a point that, even when seeing logical truths that lay before Them in the form of the allegories in black and white, the Masses believe the lie that comes forth out of the mouths of the deceivers rather than what They see and read for Themselves.

In order to consider oneself enlightened, there is a basic four-part criterion or standard that must be met.

- First, you must be able to cast aside the message of darkness that you have been conditioned to accept (the lies); you must be able to perceive the true message of Light and Self.

- Secondly, you must also be able to accept that message in its' purity, despite the fact that all your life you have been taught to directly oppose it by exercising faith in lies. At this time you must also be able to practice, exercise, and work to evolve and empower Self as well as strive for true and complete Self-Liberation along with the ability to truly exercise free will.

- Thirdly, you must reach a state, or point, where you are able to profess the true message verbally amongst friend and foe alike, bravely rejecting the lies of religion openly, with the knowledge that the Truth shall indeed set you free from the bondage(s) of deception.

- Fourth, you must be able to openly and genuinely promote the message of Truth, under the Universal Fellowship of Light, to all those seeking, or already treading, the Path of Enlightenment. This promotion of Truth can be applied in many forms such as direct work in the Temples, donations of food or other material support(s), monetary donations, volunteering for building projects, study groups, rites, exercise classes, etc. as well as official, clerical, and/or administrative work.

Presently, the author will present one of the most rudimentary of all religious teachings that is deceitfully used for the purpose of instilling the idea and belief that each individual is a corrupt 'sinner', beginning at the point of birth, due to a supposed 'original sin' which took place during the onset of creation. This story, in the way it is commonly presented and taught to the Masses, also reinforces the macabre idea that each individual should willingly choose to be completely subservient and obedient to a supposed omnipotent 'GOD' despite the obvious despotism attributed to him within the allegories in which he appears.

The author uses the allegory from the Holy Bible and also discusses the story in allegorical form himself. Please note that the author, though it might seem so, is not asking the reader to choose either side, as presented in the allegory; rather, the author points the reader to Truth; that is, the Enlightenment of Self as the Most High God and Self-Liberation as the true way to exercise free will as a living-god. The story presented is one alluding to just that, although man's religion has blinded its' followers to this fact.

Religious Origin of Sin

The Masses are told that GOD, YHWH, or Jehovah in English, created one man (Adam) and one woman (Eve). For the purpose of this illustration, the author will use the names as set forth in the King James Version of the Holy Bible although the reader is reminded to review the definition of the Gods as set forth by the author in the first chapter of this text.

The Book states that Adam and Eve were forbidden from eating the fruit of the Tree of Knowledge of Good and Evil. Jehovah informed the pair that at the time they might eat from that particular tree, they would surely die. See Genesis, Chapter 2.

The author here notes that the text of the Book sets forth that there was a second tree in the middle of the garden, the Tree of Life, which apparently, at first instance, was not forbidden from being enjoyed by Adam and Eve seeing as it was not expressly forbidden for them to eat from that tree as it was the other.

In Chapter Three the religious leaders teach that Lucifer approached Eve in the form of a Serpent (the ancient symbol of knowledge/wisdom). They teach that he then enticed her, lied to her, accused Jehovah before her, and caused Eve to commit the 'original sin' that would later be handed down to each human conceived thereafter. It is then commonly taught, and believed, that Eve caused Adam to sin also and the pair was displaced from the Garden forever due to their disobedience to Jehovah.

It is in verses six and seven where Eve takes the fruit of the Tree of Knowledge and gives it to Adam and causes him to eat it. It is in verse twenty-three where the pair are banished from the Garden by Jehovah. Between verse six and twenty-three are seventeen verses that are of significant and material nature to those who seek Truth and Light. Despite the existence of these material verses, almost all religious teachers act with deception by consciously disregarding many, if not all, of these verses. Almost always they will purposely disregard verse twenty-two because they lack the ability to include this verse into their lie in a manner that remains reasonable to those they deceive. This one verse causes the deceivers' entire deception and manipulation of this particular allegory to easily be seen as an outright lie.

The author does not request that the reader take his word for anything written in this chapter. That is what the deceivers do; they ask for your faith in what they contend to know rather than asking you to go within and find answers for yourself in order that you will know instead of merely believe. The author asks only that you would read the book of Genesis, Chapters Two and Three, from the King James Version of the Holy Bible; or, in the alternative, Google, "King James Bible/Genesis/Chapters 2 and 3" in order that you might study, reason, and think for yourself.

The author here plays the roll of Lucifer; thereby by allowing his thoughts, writings, and Light to become the bridge between your 'lower nature' (which is inclined to slavery through belief in the lie) and your 'higher nature' (which is inclined to freedom and mastery of Self through the pursuit of Light by way of intelligent and cognizant thought as well as through conscious disobedience to the ideal referred to as Jehovah).

The Bridge of Light

First, the author asks the reader to ascertain what the Serpent, or Lucifer, actually said to Eve. In fact, the first encounter between Lucifer and Eve takes place in an interrogative form rather than a declarative form. Lucifer ASKS: "... [a]nd he said unto the woman, Yea, hath [Jehovah] said, ye shall not eat of every tree of the garden?" Genesis, 3:1

The author here pauses to highlight the first of many important points. Note that Lucifer did not set out to tell Eve anything nor give her instruction. He did not demand anything or give her orders (as one might do to a slave, underling, or being that needs to be taught); rather, Lucifer addressed her as an equal; that is, upon the level. A God does not converse with a slave, he directs them and issues orders; however, Lucifer did not take this route. This is a first clue as to Eve's true status in the scope of the allegory. Lucifer questioned Eve, and expected not an obedient act, but a cognizant answer and an interaction with her on a higher level of thought than she had apparently yet to experience with Jehovah. This is yet another element of evidence as to her true nature, or status, amongst the two Gods, Lucifer and Jehovah. For was she not created in the image of the Gods? This interaction with Lucifer apparently caused Eve to unwittingly employ her latent ability to reason and cognize. Eve apparently had this latent ability even if it had, up until then, lain dormant within her and she was not aware of its presence.

So Lucifer appealed to the very ability at Eve's core that even she herself might not have been aware of: her ability to think and know. If she herself was not aware of this ability it is obvious that Lucifer was well aware of it, for why else would a superior being address another in conversation on an equal level if that other (Eve) had not the necessary ability to reason in order to engage in the cognizant dialogue? Instantly, Eve was transformed and submerged into intelligent dialogue with Lucifer as, through his questioning, he had lit the Flame of Knowledge within her.

In verses two and three, Eve reiterates the order that Jehovah had spoken (evidencing her ability for memory function), ending with Jehovah's promise that her life would be forfeit if she ate from the Tree of Knowledge.

Lucifer further appeals to Eve's reasoning and cognizance as well as her deductive abilities and to the very core of her being where she was subconsciously aware that she had been made in the image of the Gods and was like them. Lucifer tells her: "Ye shall not surely die: For [Jehovah] doth know that in the day Ye eat thereof, then your eyes shall be opened, and Ye shall be as gods, knowing good and evil." Genesis, 3:4-5

With His words, Lucifer gave Eve the reassurance that to 'know' made her like Jehovah. As the Flame of Knowledge had already been sparked, the text states: "And when [Eve] saw that the tree was good... and that it was pleasant... and a tree to be desired to make [Her] wise, she took of the fruit thereof, and did eat, and gave also unto her husband... and he did eat." Genesis, 3:6

In verse seven, the pair first become aware of themselves (their 'Selfs') as individual beings, separate and apart from the Nature around them. "And the eyes of them both were opened, and they knew that they were naked; and they sewed fig leaves together, and made themselves aprons." Genesis, 3:7

This was their first step into Light, the first fruit of their inclination to assume godhood. Before, they had not been aware of their nakedness because they had not yet been made aware of 'Self'. Thus, verse seven evidences the first OBVIOUS instance where the pair could think, or at least verbalize, "I AM". It is this explicit ability to say or think "I AM" that sparked the Thousand Points of Light causing them to become as the Gods.

This same instance also pictures the first OBVIOUS point where the pair were able to directly address each other without any mediation from Jehovah.

Next, the text shows Jehovah walking through the garden and Adam and Eve hide themselves from Him. Jehovah calls to Adam asking where he is. Genesis, 3:8-9.

These two verses evidence Jehovah's chauvinistic nature, as He addresses only the male, without any acknowledgement of the female whatsoever.

Adam finally resolves to answer: "...I heard thy voice in the garden, and I was afraid, because I was naked; and I hid myself." Genesis, 3:10

First, the author points out that the pair hid from Jehovah showing further the attainment of self-realization and, as a reasonable deduction, have realized that Jehovah is clothed, concealing his body, yet all-the-while, Adam and Eve had been bare before Him up to that point. Was it only that their bodies were bare or were their very spirits and essences also bare before Jehovah up until then?

Secondly, at this time the pair are obviously in possession of the required amount of cognizance to expect, or anticipate, Jehovah's reaction (feelings?) to their nakedness and they make an attempt (though futile) to hide the facts and evidence from Jehovah most likely as a ploy to avoid the reaction they have by now no doubt anticipated they would receive from him. There can be no doubt that the pair was aware that a core change had been created within themselves and they were no longer what they once were; that is, they had immersed themselves into materiality where before they were firstly spirit beings.

Next, it is important to notice that in his response to Jehovah, Adam grandly displays his newfound ability to cognize an intricate answer of his own and also displays his newfound self-realization by making this detailed response rather than a simple answer of "over here" to Jehovah's inquiry as to where Adam was. Adams response provided both an answer and a reason for that answer. "I am over here, because..."

Another point to consider is that, in answering Jehovah, Adam used the word 'I' no less than four times in his newly available predicate/subject response, thereby ascertaining for Jehovah that Adam had become aware of

'Self', aware he was separate and apart from Nature, had received Light in the form of knowledge, and had obviously made his way onto The Path through the Doctrine of Lucifer which is self-liberation by way of self-realization.

Jehovah's first address of Adam, after Adam's initial response, evidences Jehovah's anger and his knowledge that Adam, in his previous state before enlightenment, had been ignorant even of his very 'Self' and/or condition of 'Self' "...Who told thee that thou wast naked? Hast thou eaten of the tree whereof I commanded thee that thou shouldest not eat?" Genesis, 3:11

As the allegory reads, initially Jehovah first assumed that Adam had been informed of his nakedness almost surely because Jehovah knew that Adam was without the ability to cognize, or know. Somehow Jehovah, the all-knowing and self-styled most high, did not automatically know how Adam knew of his nakedness which, in and of itself, lends evidence that Jehovah is NOT all-knowing because he failed to foresee Adam and Eve's partaking of the Tree of Knowledge and even after they had partaken thereof, Jehovah failed to know what they had done until Adam's response, at which point Jehovah was then obviously forced to employ his own cognizance skills.

Jehovah displays his own ability to reason, cognize and deduce when he realized that Adam and Eve had done the unthinkable (in his eyes); that is, they disobeyed Jehovah's decree by exercising the very part of themselves that set them apart from and above all Order of Nature: Free Will.

Adam then blames the woman, Eve, for his transgression against Jehovah's decree. Genesis, 3:12.

That particular verse just might be the most famous recorded incident of a man using a woman as a scapegoat for the wrong he himself has committed. We all have done so. If you are of the faith represented in the bible, then it is the earliest act of 'demonizing' the woman and denying her of her rightful station in the Order of Nature; for the woman literally brings forth life from within and her body provides the sacred source of the continuing cycles of life. Further, woman is a direct conduit for man to receive and utilize the primeval force -the Ether- of creation; the way in which man, as a god, might bring order from chaos.

Jehovah then further shows his chauvinistic nature, where he implicitly agrees with Adam that the woman has done wrong, has caused Adam to do wrong (as if it was not his own decision made of his own volition) and thus Eve is the culprit rather than Adam: "And [Jehovah] said unto [Eve], What is this that thou hast done?" Eve then explains, by lying, that "...The Serpent [Lucifer] beguiled me, and I did eat." Genesis, 3:13

Eve there shows another act of cognizance (on the same level as the two Gods represented in the allegory) as well as free will, for Eve chose to tell Jehovah the lie, even though she knew that Lucifer had not lied to her because she did not die and she did become wise, seeing that the Tree of Knowledge was good. Her insistence that she had been beguiled in a negative manner was itself deception aimed towards Jehovah. No person lies to another whom they know without doubt will be aware of the lie. The only reason you might lie to another is because you believe you are capable of deceiving them. Thus, at this point, Eve knew she was Jehovah's equal, at least in the ability to cognize and reason thoughtfully, even though she was truly no match for him as he surely had had way more experience in the matter of self-consciousness than she.

Next, Jehovah shows, for the first time in the Book, his sadistic, despotic, and totalitarian nature as he proceeds to rain curses first upon the Serpent, and next, Adam and Eve. The entire Book is actually aimed at only two basic ethics: Love and Forgiveness, yet all interactions with Jehovah, from this first instance in the Book of Genesis, show that he is anything but forgiving and lends evidence of his bloodthirsty inclinations. Genesis, 3:14-19.

A third theme of the Book takes those two basic aims and compounds them into one: that humanity must strive to be like the Most High by trying to live the way Christ, 'GOD incarnate', demonstrated to his followers.

The author sets forth that although Jehovah intones that his pronouncements are 'curses' caused by his own omnipotence, in reality the 'curses' are merely revelations of events that would have taken place any way because they were really effects of the cause and effect scenario which Adam and Eve became consciously aware of upon their immersion into materiality. Up until the time of their enlightenment, Adam and Eve was not aware of themselves and so, did not experience the 'curses' with full consciousness (in terms of Self-Consciousness). Now that they had become aware of Self, they would begin to experience all events in the Order of Nature through the lens of Self-Consciousness.

In verse twenty-two Jehovah is having a separate and most likely private conversation with the only other being, aside from Adam and Eve, mentioned in the allegory up to that point. The other being, or God, was none other than Lucifer, who was the only other character, besides Jehovah, who was in possession of free-will in conjunction with knowledge, wisdom, and understanding. Jehovah tells Lucifer: "...Behold, the man is become as one of [U]s, to know good and evil; and now lest he put forth his hand, and take also of the tree of life, and eat and live forever:...". Genesis 3:22

Jehovah then proceeds to banish them from the garden and places before its' entrance in the East, a 'cherub', or guardian, with a flaming sword, turning every which way to keep (guard) the way of the Tree of Life. See Genesis, 3:23-24.

To consider verse twenty-two you have to... no, *you must*, know who the being with whom Jehovah was speaking really was. It is obvious that Jehovah addressed this being as an equal (one possessing like status) because Jehovah addresses the other with Truth. Jehovah clearly states: "...[Y]ou have made them like [U]s..." He does not say "like me", but explicitly states, "like us". The identity of this other being is one of the keys to access the Path of

Enlightenment and is one of the most misunderstood simply because it has been one of the most manipulated and hidden truths of the last two thousand years by none other than the 'Abrahamic-Religion(s)', en banc.

As stated previously herein, one can come to no other conclusion than that this second being, which existed equally with and alongside Jehovah, was the so-called 'Serpent'; or, to be more precise, Lucifer himself.

Anyone familiar with biblical doctrine, whether scholar or laymen, will concede that although Genesis is the first body of text, describing the creation of matter and life on Earth, the true or actual beginning, before the creation of physical matter, as well as the manipulation of that matter into life, takes place in the Gospel of John.

John 1:1-5 states: "In the beginning was the Word, and the Word was with God and the Word was God. The same was in the beginning with God. All things were made by him; and without him was not anything made that was made. In him was life; and the life was the light of men. And the light shineth in the darkness; and the darkness comprehended it not." John, 1:1-5

As you may have already deduced from the verse immediately quoted afore, whoever was in the garden arguing with Jehovah was also a God; for, in the beginning, there were only two. In Genesis, which also recounts the beginning, there again exist only two characters other than the created Adam and Eve. The answer of who the other being was is simple now that John 1:1-5 is considered; He was the 'Light of Men', the 'Light Bearer': Lucifer.

Remember, "...and the Word was with God and the Word was God." In our modern-day language we would expect to see the letter "a" to cause the text to say "...and the Word was [a] God"; however, this letter would not have been employed in ancient times because many times plurality, singularity, possession, action, etc. were made known by a variation of a common root-word and whichever variation was used would be employed in a manner so as to designate both subject and predicate without the aid of adjectives, adverbs, pro-nouns, etc.

Back to the text of the Book...

"All things were made by Him..." then, "...and without Him was not anything made that was made. In Him was life; and the life was the light of men." As such, the text provides a direct reference to the Light as being the actual creator of everything that was created rather than Jehovah actually performing the act of creating himself. This is definitely not commonly presented by the religious teachers; however, it is systematically supported by the Book of Genesis, Gospel of John and other places throughout the bible which refer to the Light.

Reading Genesis, and considering the Gospel of John, the reader should be able to deduce that Jehovah acted as a sort of architect, or planner (the idea or thought), who sent forth his desires, his thought-forms of creation, while the second God (in Whom was the light and life of man and who was the demiurge who created everything that was created), the Light Bearer (Lucifer), the Sun God, carried the plans to fruition and caused life to proceed from the created matter.

Before returning to Genesis to expose more of the commonly taught lie, the author concedes that almost all biblical students, both scholar and laymen alike, will claim that the Word, as set forth in the Gospel of John, is referring to Jesus. To say that the text can there only be referring to Jesus, and cannot be equally applied to Lucifer, is folly because:

- The beginning (John) references two Gods existing together at that time but is not specific of who the other God is and only references the second God as the Word and Light;
- Genesis, in the chapter outlining the creation of life on Earth, references only two beings of higher status than Adam and Eve, namely, Jehovah and the Serpent who every believing Christian will tell you is Lucifer (alluding to the Egyptian Serpent who had two distinct emanations existing within itself);
- John explicitly references the second God as the "light of men" (the very meaning of the title Lucifer is 'Light-Bearer' or 'One who brings light') and then goes on to explain that that same "light" is the "life of men"; and
- John explicitly states that it was this "life and light of men" that created everything that was created and that nothing created was created without that Light.

Here, the author will provide a key to the Mystery of Jesus. Jesus is none other than Lucifer disguised by man's religions in order to keep the Masses from partaking in the rites, practices and exercises of old, which would allow Them to transcend Their Material-Bodies and evolve Their Light-Bodies. Let me briefly explain: Jesus and Lucifer are characters used to describe the dual characteristics of the singular emanation of that ancient Egyptian Serpent. They are one, in the same manner that a coin is one but has two noticeably distinct 'sides'.

Yes, that is right, by worshipping Jesus, the Masses have been tricked into secretly worshipping Lucifer and, due to Their distinction and intellectual separation of the two, They are being prevented from enjoying the Doctrine of Lucifer and the Liberation of Self.

Jesus is the modern day Sun God and the Masses have been tricked into worshipping the man in the allegory rather than building the Temple of Light by use of the divine Jesus/Lucifer aspects taught by the Christ during his incarnation as the man Jesus.

Turn in your Book to Isaiah 14:12 where you will read: "O Lucifer, [B]right [M]orning [S]tar, how you have fallen from heaven..." This reference to Lucifer, as the Bright Morning Star, is also a reference to the Pentagram, which itself was also used as an ancient symbol of the planet Venus. In occult knowledge Venus is considered a feminine planet because the energies and forces, which She emanates, are considered to be 'passive'. The ancient civilizations referred to Venus as the Morning Star because it can sometimes be seen in the morning to 'rise' above the horizon before the Sun, depending upon the season.

Also of note, is that ancient civilizations worshipped a deity called Quetzcoatal, also known as the Morning Star, who was depicted in artwork as a feathered-serpent (flying dragon). Quetzcoatal was also none other than the planet Venus. The author here prods the sincere student to discover the elliptical pattern traversed by the planet Venus (and all the planets for that matter) in Her journey around the Sun. There you will find cosmic evidence of the pentagram.

Now flip your bible to Revelation 22:16 where you will read where Jesus states: "...I am the root and the offspring of David and the [B]right [M]orning [S]tar."

Flip your pages to John 8:12 and you will read where Jesus states: "...I am the light of the world: he that followeth me shall not walk in darkness, but shall have the light of life."

Do these particular scriptures not sound as though Jesus is declaring that He is the Light-Bearer? To understand, you must use the cognition you were created with and not be a blind follower of religion through faith as orthodox religion asks from you.

The author would here ask the reader to go back to Isaiah, 14:12 and read through the remainder of the verses in order to gain an insight of what the scriptures said would happen to Lucifer when he would one day become human and dwell on the Earth. Next, the author asks you to read any, or all, of the Gospels of the New Testament (Matthew, Mark, Luke, or John) to get a clear indication of what the character Jesus was put through on Earth just before his execution. Does the story of the Gospels, relating to the torture and crucifixion of Jesus, not sound like it is the literal fulfillment of what the supposed prophecy in Isaiah said would happen to Lucifer after he would fall from heaven to the Earth?

The ancient ones who took it upon themselves to hide the Truth in the bible, a *"Book of True Lies"*, were very clever not to erase the Truth altogether; but rather, to conceal it from those who would not work for it and could not rise any further than the Tree of Knowledge. They knew that to hide the Truth from the deceivers it would be necessary to hide the Truth in the very mechanism that the deceivers would employ to deceive mankind.

To take also the fruit of the Tree of Life, you must awaken from the matrix and rise above the Tree of Knowledge. The Truth is there for those who would *know*, yet the lie is all encompassing for those who simply 'believe in faith'. The concealment and the lie is the hurdle all must jump in order to become Illuminati.

Here is an exercise on paper for the inquisitive readers' mind in order that your eyes be opened that much further. In occult knowledge/doctrine the female is commonly represented by the number five (5) because when her arms and legs are spread out in standing position she has five main points as does the pentagram; these points are Her arm, head, second arm, leg and second leg. The male is commonly represented by the number six (6) because when his arms and legs are spread out in standing position he has six main points as does the hexagram; these points are His arm, head, second arm, leg, penis and second leg. Further, the creation of mankind in general, is biblically reported to have taken place on the "Sixth-Day".

Within the bible, in the Book of Revelation, it states that the mark of the beast will be *the number of a man*. Again, understanding that the letter "a" would not have been used in the same manner that the interpreters wrote out this particular verse we could also say that the verse should have been interpreted to say that the mark of the beast will be *the number of man*, leaving out the "a".

On a sheet of blank paper write out the letters A thru Z vertically down the left-hand side of the page. Next to the letter A write the number 6, next to B write the number 12, next to C write 18, next to D write 24, and so forth and so on, increasing incrementally by six with each letter until you reach the letter Z which should have the number 156 next to it. Refer to Illustration 2-A.

In another area of the page write the words MARK OF BEAST vertically. Next to each of these letters write the corresponding number from your previously detailed letter/number chart described afore. Now add these grouped numbers (the ones next to the words MARK OF BEAST only). True to scripture, you will reach the sum of 666.

Do the same thing with the word COMPUTER. Again, you will reach the sum of 666.

Almost any individual considering themselves a follower of any of the 'Abrahamic-Religions' will acknowledge that they believe the mark of the beast, as prophesied in Revelation, will take place by use of the computer and identification devices inserted into the skin of humans for the purpose of numbering or counting the population as well as buying and selling goods.

Now perform this exercise using the name Jesus. What sum have you reached?

Finally, perform the exercise one more time using the title Lucifer. What sum have you reached?

Remember, you know that Lucifer means Light-Bearer. You also know that in the Book, Jesus himself declares he is the light of the world that gives life. He is the Sun God. He is Lucifer who saved mankind by opening their eyes in the allegory of Genesis. In this manner he is the savior.

In keeping with Our original intention of the promotion of Truth, We must admit that Lucifer is none other than the Egypto-Christian version of Ra (the left Eye) while Jesus represents Horus (the right Eye).

Now back to Genesis...

Jehovah is complaining to Lucifer how the man and woman had been caused to become like them. Jehovah punishes Adam and Eve for their ascension and banishes them from the garden in order to prevent them from partaking of the Tree of Life and living forever. If Jehovah had really cared for them, why would he have taken away from them the real possibility of immortality just as they ascended to equal status with Him? Was Jehovah fearful of the creations new status or was he simply in a murderous rage and simply sought to ensure that

A- 6	Q- 102	M 78	C 18	J 60	L 72
B- 12	R- 108	A 6	O 90	E 30	U 126
C- 18	S- 114	R 108	M 78	S 114	C 18
D- 24	T- 120	K 66	P 96	U 126	I 54
E- 30	U- 126	O 90	U 126	S 114	F 36
F- 36	V- 132	F 36	T 120		E 30
G- 42	W- 138	B 12	E 30		R 108
H- 48	X- 144	E 30	R 108		
I- 54	Y- 150	A 6			
J- 60	Z- 156	S 114			
K- 66		T 120			
L- 72					
M- 78					
N- 84					
O- 90					
P- 96					

Illustration 2-A

Adam and Eve would eventually die for their audacity of becoming what they were created with the potential to be, which was, *like* Him and the other God, the Serpent?

From the allegory, as presented within the Book, it is plain that Lucifer was desirous for the creation to come into their rightful state, as gods, even though Jehovah sought to keep them subservient to Him and was even childishly angry that they were made aware of 'Self' and knew they were naked.

Jehovah wished the creation to remain as mindless automatons, whereas Lucifer desired to share creation and nature with the gods (humans) he himself had created at the behest of Jehovah.

As such, Lucifer was the true benefactor of mankind (the creation) for He knew well that when He had created us, He did so in the image of the Gods; that is, with the ability to think, reason, cognize and, above all, to exercise free will outside of the Law(s) of Nature. Lucifer knew that by using his own essence in the process of creating mankind, He had actually made them gods and goddesses. Lucifer was aware that the creation was nothing less than the Goddess and God, the Primary and Secondary Deities, incarnated or transformed into a new form: male and female.

Out of all creation (Nature) the man and the woman were the only created things which could separate themselves from certain natural laws after becoming aware of 'Self' and could exert their own desires and will into Nature. They were able to use the very laws and forces of Nature in a manner so as to bring about their own will and desires because they were, and still are, the Goddess and God incarnate.

There is also another particularly important lesson taught in the allegory just gone over; however, the author will not spend much time here going into it. The author will say however, that the important reason why Lucifer initiated knowledge in the woman first, rather than the man, was because the woman was further advanced physically, mentally and psychologically and more than likely was in possession of a more highly evolved/advanced Light-Body than the man. Further, unlike the man, the woman enjoys direct contact with the Primary Deity whereas the man requires a conduit (woman) to receive that same contact.

Readers, how strong are you? How enlightened are you? Have you been able to think and reason as you advanced through this chapter or has it caused you to submerse your mind even that much deeper into the religious teachings you have been deceived with your entire life? Maybe some of you were already aware of the Truth presented here?

Now, it is one thing to think it or know it, and to allow that knowledge to remain hidden within your mind and heart; but, have you the courage and strength to confess it openly, aloud, then turn and teach it to others who seek enlightenment along The Path?

Throughout history, the 'horned-deities' have always symbolized Light as well as the feminine and/or masculine aspect of the Sun Gods and Sun Goddesses. These deities have been known by humanity as Ra, Osiris, Ammon-Ra, Isis, Pan, the Viking Helmet, Loki, Hiram-Abiff, Jesus (symbolized as the Ram caught in the brush by his horns as Abraham was preparing to sacrifice Isaac), Baphomet, Nimrod, Ishtar, Statue of Liberty. All these names and instances represent the true state of the Goddess and God in the allusion of the horned-deities (i.e., the goat/ram/dragon).

The author sets forth that if you are able to speak the following statement aloud to another individual whom you know to be oppressed by the lies of religion, and mean it wholeheartedly, then you have truly loosed the chains of bondage that accompany man's religion and the adoration of Jehovah. If however, you cannot say the following statement, you are still within the cage of man-made religion but, if you can find the courage to practice this simple exercise/technique (saying it aloud repeatedly until you mean it and live it each day) then you will have taken your first step(s) upon the Path of Enlightenment. Light will then begin to be drawn to you and you will begin to retain this Light as it is drawn towards the magnetism and power of the words you speak aloud:

"I confess that Lucifer, in all forms, is the True God, emanated into matter, and the benefactor of creation while Jehovah is the unseen Secondary Deity which projects the Spiritual Light of the Goddess. Furthermore, it was Jehovah who wished to keep the creation in darkness as mindless automatons. I confess that Jesus and Lucifer are One and the teachings of the Christ are none other than the Doctrines of Lucifer, the Universal Doctrine of Light."

If you have just spoken these last words aloud, in a bold and powerful manner, so as to defy that which you have been conditioned to obey, you may be experiencing a type of euphoria or feeling of lightness in your body and spirit. This lightness is the metaphorical chain of spiritual bondage and darkness being cast aside and the first bit of the indwelling of spiritual light coming into your being. Your very essence is being lightened as the heavy chains of indoctrination begin to disappear. The difference now is that you are aware and conscious of it, what it is, and what is happening; whereas before, you did not know these chains were present and weighing you down. Enjoy the feeling of the beginning of the Liberation of Self. Bask in the Light of Lucifer. You are to become one of Us.

Spooky, is it not?

Words for Thought

The author's thoughts here are based solely upon the allegory as presented within the Holy Bible and as such, should only be considered as that; as thoughts on the allegory as presented in that specific version of the many allegories of the creation of life.

Placing the forbidden Tree of Knowledge of Good and Evil into the midst of the Garden of Eden at first glance does not seem to be so terrible an idea, even considering the fact that it was forbidden to partake of the tree's fruit and even if you consider that the man and woman, in their state of *unknowing* existence were (at least early on) incapable of truly distinguishing any benefits or penalties which might coincide with the eating from any one tree or another.

The first *evil* in the plan for creation came when Jehovah explicitly, and intentionally, brought the very existence of the Tree of Knowledge to the forefront of Adam and Eve's attention. Was this simply oversight, a mistake, on behalf of the supposed all-knowing Jehovah? Or, was it part of his original intention to cause the tree's existence to be directly centered within the man and woman's daily thoughts and considerations? If so, how vile of an act was this?

Consider a mother in today's society who places a plate or bowl containing approximately one hundred cookies onto the center of the kitchen or dining room table. Next the mother calls the children, along with four or five of their visiting friends, into the dining room and tells them, "I just finished baking all these chocolate-chip cookies and they are ready to be eaten. They are fresh and warm, but I baked them using a bit of poison that will make you really sick after a few hours. So you are not allowed to eat these chocolate-chip cookies even though you will not get sick right away."

"Why?" asks little Johnny.

"Because I said so; I am your mother and you will obey me. If you eat these fresh baked cookies, you will eventually get sick. Now, I'm going shopping and I'll be gone all day long."

In this short scenario it seems absurd that the parent would do and say these things to children who most certainly are not going to be able to fully understand the penalties of eating the cookies; further, it seems absurd that the parent would go through such measures simply to exert authority over the children. Why did the mother in the scenario entice them in the manner that she did? Why did she not only emphasize what was supposed to take place (the penalty) but also emphasized the truth about the cookies; that is, that they were warm, fresh, and ready to be eaten. She thereby let it be known that, despite the penalty, the cookies would also be good to the children and she therefore actually caused them to desire the treats.

In the allegory of Adam and Eve that exactly was the precise method used to bring the man and woman into the state of their true being or nature. To make them conscious, like the Gods, they had to be enticed and Jehovah did just that. Later, the same Jehovah blames the Serpent for what Jehovah also had a hand in causing.

Like the Truth related openly by the Serpent, today the effective route to cause modern humanity to become what we truly are is Truth through the Luciferian Doctrine.

Next, the mother in the scenario went so far as to lay down the ground-work of when the children could commit the betrayal. Remember? She said, "...you will obey me.", then she said, "I'm going shopping... I'll be gone all day long."

What is your personal opinion of the mother in the scenario?

By exerting authority over Adam and Eve, Jehovah did the same thing that the mother in the scenario did to the kids. In the scenario, would you suppose the mother there would be ignorant to the fact of what her kids, and some of the visiting friends, would surely do once she had abandoned them for shopping? Or, would you expect her to at least be aware of her children's nature as you yourself are aware of your own children's nature. So, obviously, Jehovah too knew what they would do. Did Jehovah possess the ability to create matter and the universe, yet still be so naive? It is doubtful.

Knowing that the kids could not, or would not, abstain from at least trying a cookie, why would the mother go so far as to create such a penalty for eating the cookies? The mother might have simply said, "here are some chocolate-chip cookies, eat them.", and then allowed the penalty to proceed in due course. But no, for the mother, that is not the point. She wants to inflict the penalty upon the children and then desires an escape route from the responsibility and/or guilt. She wants to say, "Yes, I did this to you, and you now have to suffer, but it is all your fault kids, because I both warned and ordered you not to eat them."

Would not making the cookies without the poison and penalty been better? For either way, it takes the same amount of effort to make the goodies with or without the poison (curse). So, either there is benefit in the penalty of the allegorical Tree (it made them *like* the two Gods) OR the one God was despotic.

As surely as you think the mother's actions were atrocious, so did Jehovah act in this very same manner.

Yes, Jehovah warned the man and woman, but it came in a manipulative manner so as to bring about a desired effect. For, by placing the tree into the very center of their minds, Jehovah placed before an inferior being a 'bowl of cookies' he knew would not be left untouched by the 'kids'. The author uses the words inferior being because an individual free-will choice had not yet occurred or been made by the humans in the allegory.

So the warning was, in fact, a camouflaged enticement by Jehovah to goad them into eating from the tree in order to bring about Jehovah's desired intention for the material beings: DEATH.

Is this not so? For as soon as they had eaten of the tree, in comes Jehovah to rebuke them and pronounce their impending death. The audacity of Jehovah was that he made it seem as though they had caused the death sentence when in reality it is plain that it was he who had caused the tree to be made to bear that penalty. And what other conclusion or outcome did Jehovah truly intend for the couple other than death? None, for the text even states that Jehovah was aware that they could indeed become immortal by eating of the Tree of Life, so he therefore banished them from the garden, effectively mandating their demise.

Consider next that it was in Adam and Eve's very makeup, as created, to disobey. The man, as well as the woman, was intentionally made in the image of God and this fact would necessitate their ability to act of their own free will and accord (even unto disobedience) for without free-will and the ability to exercise it, the humans would no longer be an image of God; but rather, a mere animal controlled by the laws of creation and boundaries of Nature along with the Group-Spirit.

The WILL (free-will) which first existed as that feminine aspect of force or energy, and which first caused the agglomeration of matter, is the very essence existing in man and woman causing him or her to be living-gods. As such, it was Adam and Eve's purpose, as created, to cause a descent into material existence through their free-will choice of disobedience to Jehovah. It is the very nature of the human to desire greatness. The infant, while crawling, views other beings such as itself walking in an upright manner and perceives a unique interaction among those whose spinal columns are vertical rather than horizontal. Because that infant is an incarnation of the thoughts, will and desire of Deity into material form, it understands that it is one of these upright beings also and begins to be like the grownups. This same aspiration is played out time and time again and can next be played out when the child wants to talk; next when he wants to learn to potty; again when he learns to feed himself.

Now consider every orthodox religion. If you are familiar with the Christian doctrine, as taught to the Masses, you must realize and come to terms with the fact that the most socially accepted version of that doctrine contains the two following mandates:

- The ONE GOD physically incarnated into Jesus where He displayed for humanity an example of a sinless and perfect life so as to become a ransom for the penalty of sin; and,
- Each individual must believe that Jesus died for their sins and paid their spiritual debt and each must be inclined to be like that Savior in manner, attitude and approach to the temptations of the flesh.

There you have it, the Great Dichotomy. If the original sin, which warranted death, was for Adam and Eve to desire to be like the Gods, why is it a mandate of orthodox Christianity to be like 'GOD' whose image has become the character Jesus.

In this light, the pair actually fulfilled their intended purpose as did the Light-Bearer. Why else bestow such title (Light-Bearer) to the very one that would be the bearer of light, as well as material life, if that not be the desired outcome?

The rhetorical question here is: "Why the anger, hostility and punishment (in the form of curses) from Jehovah when each character in the allegory of Genesis, Chapter Three, fell perfectly in line with the boundaries and natures of the roles they were obviously created, or intended, to take on?"

Could it be, that the installation of having fear of the Gods was strategically placed into the allegory so as to ensure that the Masses would personally choose to forsake the Doctrine of Light and surrender to the Doctrines of Jehovah; thereby ensuring the authority of the orthodox religions and the administrators of those religions?

CHAPTER THREE

ORIGIN OF ORTHODOX RELIGION

"We see a great world before us, and all the wondrous things it contains. But in fact, we see all that, only within us. In other words, there is a kind of photographic machine in the back of our brain, which portrays every-thing that we see, and there is nothing out-side of us."

-Baal Ha Sulam
Preface to the Book of Zohar

If the reader were to seek to understand the way in which spiritual and intellectual movements develop in humanity, he or she would first be re-quired to realize that nothing that humans do or think concerns, first and foremost, anything other than the satisfaction of their feelings and personal needs or, in some instances, an escape from one form of pain or another. No matter how noble human striving and productivity may appear, or display themselves to be, feeling and longing are the true forces behind any motion of such striving or productivity.

It is fear, first and foremost, that awakens the ideas of religion in the more primitive or backwards peoples. Fear of hunger, wild animals, illness, unexplained natural phenomena and death are but a few examples of this driving force called fear. Since these persons, being primitive, will almost always lack any understanding of cause and effect in the universe or their immediate environment, the human creates within his or her mind a super-natural being, a GOD, more or less like itself and in its image, on whose will, action or punishment depends the experiences which the human fears. The believers or followers of this created being, or GOD, then hopes to win the favor of said being by deeds, sacrifice, faith, observance, dedication or mercy according to the tradition of the race, nation, religion or doctrines. These deeds, sacrifices, faiths, observances, dedications or mercies are believed by these followers to appease said being or cause his disposition toward them to be more favorable in one way or another. This is known as the religion of fear.

How many orthodox religions of the so-called modern era are based, at least in part, on the fear of its adherents? No matter the perceived advance-ment or evolution of such a religion, a religion of fear can never be any more advanced than the primitive persons and fears which caused its origin in the first place or, in the cases of certain age-old religions still practiced today, the followers who continue to perpetuate its' dogma. Even when such a religion develops into a doctrine which on the surface may seem to be new or different, or where the religion adopts a more current or seemingly more relaxed dogma, the inability for such a religion to evolve beyond its' original state of primitiveness is due to the very emotion which created such a belief system in the first place; that is, the very same fear that created the doctrine. It is that very same fear that is required to uphold and perpetuate the doctrines relativity, effectiveness and authority. If any follower of said doctrines were to suddenly find themselves without this emotion, which substantiated the doctrine in the first instance, then that doctrine would become void of relativity, effectiveness or authority over, or for, that particular individual. As such, this doctrine must necessarily perpetuate the advancement of some form of that original fear, no matter how it is reinvented or reinterpreted, if it intends to maintain its relevance and authority.

This religion of fear necessitates considerable stabilization by and through the formation of some form of priestly class which claim to be the mediator(s) between the religions followers and the being or GOD they fear. This role as mediator automatically brings about some form of attainment of power and authority over that doctrine's followers who are not a part or member of the priestly class. Almost always, the mediators will claim that their authority stems from, or was bestowed upon them by, the being that is feared. Many times leaders, despots, governments or the privileged classes, being already in some position of power which is maintained by other means, will combine the function of the mediating priesthood with its' own secular rule in order to further secure its' rule and authority; similarly, sometimes a simple alliance may exist between political powers and the mediators whenever like interests exist. An example of the combination of political powers and the mediating priesthood can be identified in the relationships long enjoyed by the Roman Catholic Church and the ruling Royal Families of Europe in the past two-thousand years.

The other source of orthodox religious development can be found located in the feelings of morality, need for guidance, love and assistance in time of distress experienced by fathers, mothers, as well as leaders of the community. These feelings normally present themselves due to the fact that even great leaders and parents are mortal and fallible, making mistakes which sometimes affect the entire community negatively. The longing and desire for guidance, love and succor is the very stimulus which easily calls forth the idea of a social and/or moral concept of Deity. This moral concept of Deity would be the GOD of Providence who simultaneously protects, rewards, punishes and makes decisions for its followers. In this religion, GOD both loves and provides for the life and people who are of His chosen race or tribe; or, in some instances, the whole of humanity. This is the GOD who is the comforter in times of unhappiness and unsatisfied longing as well as the punisher of the morally corrupt and the protector of the souls of its dead followers. This religion is known as the religion of social morality.

Sometimes, as in the Judeao-Christian doctrine, the religion of fear will develop into the religion of social morality, however, this should not be considered an evolution, per se, of the religion of fear because even in the religion of social morality, the fear of incurring the punishment of the doctrines' GOD is still prevalent as is the loss of a supposed benefit, which is normally the gift of immortality after the physical death of the individual follower. Punishment is usually some form of torture of the soul throughout eternity. Principally, the religions of so-called civilized peoples will develop into the religion of social morality and will itself contain and disguise its' foundations in the religion of fear through one form of rhetoric or another.

It would be quite difficult to find a religion of fear that has not the underlying goal of some form of morality as its' pinnacle and, likewise, one would be hard-pressed to find a religion of social morality that does not promote morality, and the fear of GOD, as the only alternative to punishment by that GOD. The only true difference from one orthodox doctrine to the next is its' emphasis on fear or morality; all are mixed forms. What all forms of these orthodox religions have in common is an anthropomorphic character who is thought to literally be GOD. Once again, as in all forms of man-made religion, the idea of GOD, in the image of MAN, is present.

Only exceptionally gifted individuals or especially noble communities rise essentially above these levels. Only Illuminati, those truly enlightened individuals, are able to rise to the third level of spirituality even if this level is seldom found in a pure state or form. Illuminati recognize neither dogma nor the GOD made in the image of MAN even where We might utilize the picture or ideal of the human (or human-like) form to teach, and sometimes disguise, this third level of spirituality. We see not merely that image, but the concept or ideal represented by such image.

Here, we will designate this third level of spirituality as the Universal Doctrine of Light. Our Universal Doctrine is hard to clarify for those who are not one of Us since those who are unenlightened cannot and will not experience it. The Universal Doctrine does not involve an anthropomorphic understanding of Deity because We know that We are the Deity; that is, the Godform enclosed within the Material-Body. Illuminati feel and know the vanity of desires and aims which are based on individualism rather than those intended for the benefit of the fold of Illuminati. Likewise, We are able to feel, see and understand the noble and marvelous order of architecture found in, and revealed by, Nature as well as the world of inner-thought and imagination. To put it plainly, the thing that you are after is already here, within you.

Illuminati know that the hive destiny is more important than individual destiny, except perhaps where individual destiny is used to further or advance the existence, unity and significance of Illuminati or Our agenda. We know that otherwise, individual destiny is but an imprisonment within the muddy vesture of decay.

Indications or examples of the Universal Doctrine of Light can be found even in early levels of human development such as the Prophets, Buddhism, Taoism, Hinduism and other Eastern Doctrines of the Orient.

The religious geniuses of all times, such as Democritus, Christ, Leonardo da Vinci, Albert Pike, Adam Weishaupt, Eliphas Levi, Galileo, Confucius and Pythagoras, to name but a few, have all been highly distinguished by their advancement of the Universal Doctrine which recognizes neither dogma nor any GOD made in MAN's image. Consequently, there can be no church, in the most readily accepted definition, whose chief doctrines are based on the Universal Doctrine. A church of the Universal Doctrine can only be realized if the word is defined as a building where like-minded Illuminati gather in order to promote the ideas and understanding of that doctrine or, a place or area where the rites of the same are acknowledged and put into practice.

For these reasons, We find that it was precisely and solely among those considered to be the heretics of all the ages that are found persons inspired by the Universal Doctrine. Often these Enlightened Ones appeared to their contemporaries to be atheists, Satanists, or worse; however, in a few cases, they were revered as saints.

The reader may wonder how it is that the Universal Doctrine can be communicated from human to human if it does not lead Us to a definite conception of GOD or to a particular theology. Illuminati know and understand that it is the most important, and perhaps only, function of the seven arts and sciences to arouse and keep alive the feeling(s) of the Universal Doctrine in those who are receptive.

Neither the religion of fear nor the religion of social morality can therefore have any hold on Illuminati. Some GOD who rewards and punishes is for Us unthinkable because it is the human who acts in accordance to some inner and outer necessity, desire or act of will. To believe in that GOD would be to express the idea that even We, Illuminati, are but mindless automatons who are as little responsible for any action, decision or choice We make as is an inanimate object for the movements which it makes at the hands of Nature, humanity or animal. To believe in the idea of a GOD who interferes with the sequences of events in a world of cause and effect, or with Our free-will choice(s), would be to wholly cause the idea of Our status as Illuminati to be moot.

As Illuminati, We understand that the ethical behavior of humanity or society would be better were it based upon sympathy, education and social-relationships; further We understand that this ethical behavior actually requires no support from religion and is actually better realized without the dogmas of religion or GOD. The plight of Illuminati, as well as the Masses, would indeed be in a sad and deteriorated state if the fear of punishment, or hope of rewards after death, were required to keep Us, or Them, in order.

When the subject is thus considered, it is no wonder, and quite natural, that the orthodox religions have always fought against science, art and Illuminati in order to prevent or curb the loss of their power and authority over their followers. Likewise, it is no wonder why those who have promoted the Universal Doctrine have historically been persecuted by these same religions.

Religion and Forgiveness

It is the very ideals of organized religion, that is, religious doctrines consisting of the idea of the forgiveness of sin by a higher being than the Self, which are to blame for mankind's current state of mental, moral and physical decay.

The idea that a person can cause harm to another person or themselves and receive 'mercy' by the 'grace' of a Creator is the very thought-pattern that prevents a person from learning from his mistakes and errors. One must be held accountable, to the degree that he or she is forced to consider the fact that he or she messed up. Further, this same individual must be able to use intelligent thought to determine what exactly was 'right' or 'wrong' about their actions and/or decision making processes.

Any belief system which allows the wrong-doer to continue to act inconsiderately, while FREELY excusing his or her actions, does not, and cannot, promote the positive growth of the individual.

It is in the moment that the wrong-doer becomes aware that he or she has done some wrong or caused some harm when true enlightenment begins to take place. When he or she realizes that they are the cause of their wrongdoing, rather than some idea of a sinister devil, that the beginning of true forgiveness can start to take place.

Obviously, the individual would first be required to acknowledge the harm he or she has caused no matter whether that harm is to another person or to his or herself. Secondly, one would be required to acknowledge that there can be no forgiveness if it takes any form other than self-forgiveness. This is because, no act of a supposed Creator God can ultimately, and with true finality, bestow upon that person a real sense of forgiveness. Each person must find that sense of forgiveness within his or her own Self and must be able to accept it once it is found.

We are not perfect in our actions. We make mistakes; yet, it is these very mistakes, or 'sins' as they are called, that make the Universal Doctrine perfect in and of itself. It is our imperfections that force some (not all) persons to strive to achieve perfection. The question of whether this perfection can actually be attained or not is for the individual thinker to determine for his or herself and the author will not attempt to make that consideration here.

When the thinker begins to see that the action of requesting forgiveness from a higher being than his or herself is pointless, as it does nothing to change or alter the thought-pattern that created the 'sin' any way, then that person has truly found a Point of Light that will allow for the beginning of illumination of the entire concept of 'Self'.

At this time, Self is the highest consciousness that the Godform has attained to in the vast majority of people living; however, this cannot be taken lightly because it is that very awareness of Self, to be able to say I AM, that grants Us the ability to become living-gods and unite Our consciousness with the Godform.

When a person commits some act or makes a decision that negatively affects either themselves or another individual, that is, an act that negates the eminent or future exercise of free-will, it is then that he or she must act within his or her capabilities as a living-god to forgive themselves or others when necessary. If the 'I AM' is GOD, and the individual is in unity with the Godform, then the forgiveness of Self, after committing error, is necessary for the further development of god-consciousness.

Keep in mind that it is a person's ability to unite the Self with the Godform, along with the ability to choose whether or not to commit 'sin', which makes that person a living-god. It is also a person's ability to know or feel when they have done wrong, and to chastise and forgive themselves for that wrong, which further sets humankind apart from all of Nature as living-gods.

Certain religions, whose GODS are considered to be the source of forgiveness, are the very religions whose gods are to blame for the error of 'sin' in the first place and therefore those GODS can, in reality, be no other entity than the individual human Self. If an individual has to rely on a GOD to forgive him or her for a supposed 'sin', then that religion is effectively removing from each individual his or her inherent godhood, or sense of divinity, and erroneously bestowing it upon that supposed GOD. This is because it takes from that individual the very fundamental acknowledgement that he or she is 'GOD' and instead attributes the sense of godhood onto, or into, one or more central anthropomorphic figures. These persons, each individual Self, thereby lose singular spirit identity and becomes enmeshed in the darkness of the group-spirit. They then become easily controlled by the authorities of that religion in the same manner that the animals are governed by group-spirits and are unable to act outside the laws set forth by the group-spirit and Nature. Their individual inner-light is thereby effectively dimmed or, in some instances, darkened altogether.

In this manner, such a religion causes disharmony and a dichotomy within its followers because it is mankind's subconscious knowledge of his or her godhood that makes them able to state: "I am this...; I want that...; I can do this...; or I will do that..." A conflict is created because there exists within each person the natural inclination towards the realization that the individual soul is 'GOD'. Such conflict creates disharmony and is aimed at the prevention of unity with the Godform, which is the the true and highest goal of each individual lifetime.

If a god were prevented from acknowledging that he or she erred, that he or she is responsible for the forgiveness and atonement of that error and that he or she is responsible for learning from the error in order to prevent further 'sin', then he or she is no longer a god, no longer in possession of freedom and he or she would be caused to become a slave to the god of whatever particular religion they seek forgiveness from.

Are you hearing this?

It is the *Universal Doctrine of Light* that allows the Self to remain in unity with the Godform and allows for the possession of conscious awareness of the same. When the living-god is aware that all mistakes, errors and 'sins' are attributable to his or herself, rather than some evil influence or force, and that all forgiveness and atonement for these mistakes, errors or 'sins' are likewise attributable to none other than his or herself, rather than some holy influence or GOD, then he or she is Illuminati. When that awareness is attained, then can the living-god deal appropriately, accordingly, respectfully and fairly with all other living-gods; that is, upon the level. The powers, energies and focus which would have otherwise been spent upon, or attributed to, some outlying Creator-God, can then be used to further the development of the Light-Body in order that the Godform might finally, once and for all, slip that muddy vesture of decay.

For these reasons, one would do his or herself great justice if he or she were to refrain from going any place outside of Self for forgiveness of 'sins'. Rather, one must go within to seek out the questions and answers as to why such a 'sin' was committed in the first place.

The words of the Great Mother ring true: "If that which Ye seek Ye find not within, Ye shall never find it without."

CHAPTER FOUR

THE VEIL OF ISIS

*"You are united with all. You are one with
the eternal Light Itself."*

-Ernest Holmes
This Thing Called You
p. 145

Those individuals who succeed in conquering matter sufficiently enough to receive the Light from the Black Sun feel Truth intuitionally, for they are ILLUMINATED. Any inspirations manifested in or through these persons are none other than the effects of this illumination by his/her own immortal spirit.

Whether that Light of Truth illuminates him or her through intuition, inspiration, regular initiation or as a consequence of study, the method and path traced by such men as Moses, Buddha and Jesus is followed and accepted by them, even if only by inference.

How much of this illumination he or she is allowed to share with the Masses is a question of its' own. The veil covering the face of the teacher cannot be withdrawn by his or her will alone; rather, it depends also on the listeners and whether they will also choose to remove the veil that is upon their hearts.

If the minds of the Masses are blinded by the shining skin of divine Truth, even if the veil be withdrawn from the face of the teacher, that veil cannot be removed from the hearts of the Masses unless Their hearts shall turn to the Lord. The appellation Lord must not be applied to any anthropomorphized personage or deity, but rather, to the Lord as is understood in Hermetic philosophy; that is, the Lord, who is Life, and MAN. Or, as the author states elsewhere, Self as the one and true living-god.

Truth is known only by the few even though it is subconsciously realized and believed by many. This conscious possession of Truth is why We define Ourselves as separate from the Masses. Most are unwilling to withdraw the veil from Their own hearts, and in this refusal, They imagine that We who know Truth are actually blinded by Our own veil which is erroneously viewed by Them as the same veil that They themselves are blinded by. They cannot imagine seeing without it, nor can They imagine that the GOD of every exoteric religion is but an idol, a fiction, and cannot be anything more.

Just as a light shines a thousand rays in a thousand different directions, so do the numerous religions and/or belief systems seem to travel toward as many different destinations; however, just like the light, said religions and beliefs all have one central point of origin where they all diverge from the whole, the One Source. Likewise, the same are actually travelling toward the same destination and illuminate the same Truths regardless of any seeming dichotomy. This is the meaning of the authors' statement that all Paths, loosely termed as Pagan, individually exist to make up the whole of the Doctrine of Lucifer and this title Lucifer is only used within this text because the average reader will be more familiar with the meaning and implication of that title than any other non-Christian reference (i.e., a reference to that same ideal using a different title). All religions and belief systems, including atheism, have at their center the very same object in view: MAN (Self).

Rather than claiming that the GOD of religion made man in his own image, the claim should actually be inverted in order to more accurately reflect Truth. With this inversion in mind, it should be stated that man imagines the GOD of religion(s) after his own image and man has thus SET UP HIS OWN REFLECTION FOR WORSHIP. Illuminati know that man is already secretly or unknowingly worshipping Self in the practice of both orthodox as well as unorthodox religion and that this focus on Self is the whole of the Doctrine of Lucifer. To learn is to worship and simultaneously progress along ones' individual Path into godhood.

The claim that GOD made man in his own image can only be viewed by the Enlightened Ones as the Gods as explicitly defined for the purpose of this book, that is, the race of beings lower in scale than the Primary and Secondary Deities, and, at minimum, one grade or more higher than that of the humanity they created.

A close scrutiny of the 'Abrahamic-Religions' reveal at least one disturbing undercurrent of those belief systems. They all suspiciously lack any emphasis on the feminine. The puppet masters of those religions have effectively censored the feminine for centuries even though the Goddess existed in every doctrine from whence the doctrines of the 'Abrahamic-Religions' where stolen or borrowed. After investigating the Torah, Bible and Koran, one can only realize how insidiously anti-feminine the doctrines of those books are. The world has been done a great disservice by the propagation of such dangerous attitudes and, if there is any one cause of the worlds' ills, it is no doubt the legacy of the last two thousand years of the orchestrated repression of women as well as the hatred and fear of the feminine principle along with the energy and force She represents.

Descent Into Matter

The author here presents another well-known, even famous, allusion contained within the Holy Bible which most often goes wholly unnoticed and which bible scholars cannot explain away as mere coincidence due to the allusions' intricate and obvious facts. The allusion referred to here is the allusion of the crucifixion of Jesus, the Christ.

In the Gospels one will read about the trial, torture and execution of Jesus. Specifically, in Matthew (27:37), Mark (15:26), Luke (23:38) and John (19:19-20) the actual location or site of the crucifixion is detailed. The reader of these verses is informed that above, or behind, the men being executed were signs written in three languages (Latin, Hebrew and Greek) which read Jesus of Nazareth, King of the Jews.

In the Latin language this phrase would have been written in the following manner: Ieusus Nazarinus, Rexes Ieus. The author points out to the reader that the first letter of each Latin word is I. N. R. I., respectively. Clearly, this is a correct representation of these facts, as can be evidenced by the investigation of the cross which hangs in most every Roman Catholic Church.

I.N.R.I.

Illustration 4-A

If one examines the officially accepted version, or image, of the cross on which was hung the body of Jesus, there you will undoubtedly find a small representation of the above-described sign proclaiming Jesus as the King of the Jews. Now days, the sign is shortened and only the abbreviation of those Latin words is included thereon. Illustration 4-A is an accurate depiction of the image of the crucified Christ.

In order to fully understand the above described information as an allusion to a higher teaching, the author must move to a highly detailed symbol of esoteric and occult philosophy, the pentagram.

Presently the author uses this symbol as set forth by the bible-based organization, or secret-society, commonly known as the Order of the Eastern Star. The motto or slogan of this Order is: "We have seen His Star in the East and are come to worship Him."

The pentagram, along with the inverted pentagram, is a common symbol used by many religions, theologies and esoteric Paths. The inversion of the Star actually has no bearing on whether or not white-magic, black-magic or holy-magic is being performed. Neither is the inverted pentagram necessarily a denotation of Satanism even though this symbol was adopted by the Church of Satan as part of its logo. Due to the adoption of the inverted pentagram as a very popular symbol of Satanism, many people without education on the subject erroneously believe that any time the star is inverted it is done to denote the worship of, or belief in, Satan as GOD rather than the Christian form of GOD.

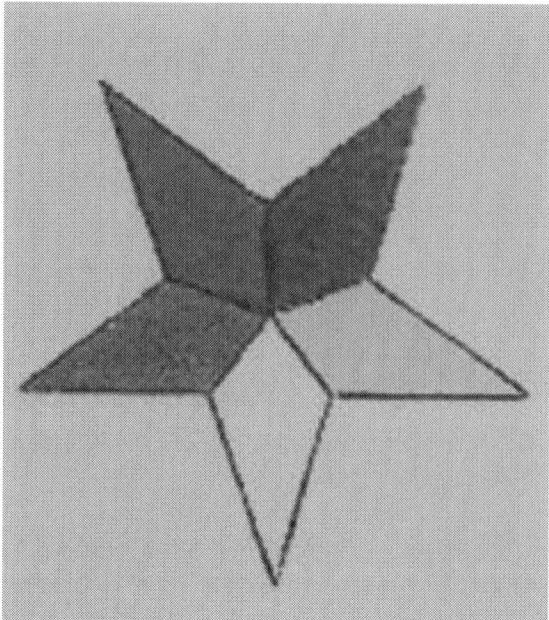

Illustration 4-B

The author will take the time to explain the single difference in the Star as used by the Order of the Eastern Star and the Star as used in most other Paths. In Illustration 4-B the adept student will notice that the inverted Star used by the Eastern Stars depicts the upper right point as being blue. In other esoteric Paths, this particular point is green and the point that is green in Illustration 4-B is blue in those other Paths.

These two points of the inverted pentagram are the only two points that will ever be seen to have their positions swapped with one another. The reason that these two points are interchangeable can only be understood by realizing that the words naming the four material elements, actually the first letters of those words, have a number value in the numerological system known as Cabbalistic Numerology.

In any school of thought presenting itself as scientific, even spiritual-science (magic), if the words naming two elements begin with the same letter and that letter has a specific number value and the number value of that letter is a key to some mathematical formula, then that letter value must be the same each time it is used or else the supposed scientific equation is nothing more than information manipulated to evidence the outcome in a manner which the scientist desires. It would be neither scientific nor credible. For this reason, because the letters are the same two letters and because the number values of those letters must necessarily be identical, the blue and green points alone are interchangeable in the pentagram.

With that notable variance explained and out of the way, the author can describe the Star itself. Each colored point of the Star corresponds to a different Element as understood within esoteric and occult tense. The color correspondences are pretty simple and self-explanatory; however, the author will list them accordingly:

Blue = Water
Red = Fire
Yellow = Air

Green = Earth

White = Spirit/Ether/Light.

As seen in the Kabbalah's Tree of Life, depicted in Illustration 5-B, the LIFE came down into matter in a zigzagged or lightning bolt pattern beginning first at the singularity (#1) and next moving right to left rather than left to right. In this same manner, the pattern of the Star is followed from right (blue) to left (red), next zigzagging across and down to lower right (yellow) then across to lower left (green) and finally to the lowest point (white).

As noted above each color represents one of the four main categories of elements, and as seen here, the Latin words for Water, Fire, Air and Earth are Iammim, Nour, Ruach, and Isbechar, respectively.

Here, the author must take the time to point out that the Latin words depicted above (to name the Elements) and the words depicted in Illustration 4-A (describing Jesus as the king of the Jewish people) have at their beginning (their initials) the same four letters: I.N.R.I. As such, not only does the Order of the Eastern Star provide a nexus between Jesus and the Eastern Star (planet Venus), as shown in their motto, but there exists a correlation between the above-noted letters also, even if they are the initials of different words.

That specifically is the point of using allegory rather than simply exposing the alluded to information outright. Allegory, as well as rhetoric, are the tools whereby the enlightened have succeeded in blinding the Masses with Light.

Below are the number values for the four letters relative to this subject as provided in the Cabbalistic numbering system. The author is not familiar with the number value for every letter of the English language; however, the number values for the letters I.N.R.I. are as follows:

$$I. = 10$$
$$N. = 50$$
$$R. = 200$$
$$I. = 10$$

Next, these number values should be added together in the following manner:

$$10 + 50 + 200 + 10 = 270.$$

Two hundred and seventy is the numerological value of the four material elements of the Blazing Star. This number has significant value in that it is also the approximate number of days required for the period of human gestation.

At first glance this might not seem to be that significant however, the fact that the human gestation period is concealed within a very important, maybe the most important, allegory of the Bible should be considered highly significant. What exactly is the allegory trying to relate to the enlightened mind? Could it be that MAN is GOD, the Secondary Deity, incarnated into the created material universe while WOMAN is the GODDESS, the Primary Deity, incarnated in like manner?

First let us consider that the pentagram, as alluded to by the allegory of the crucifixion of Jesus, represents the human and, more specifically, the fetus. Using the pentagram to symbolically represent the fetus presents an allusion to the combination of the four material elements combined with the fifth element (light/ether/spirit) to form a perfect combination whereby a Material-Body can be built in order for the Godform to experience an incarnation within matter. This analogy can be compared to the religious belief that, after the combination of the sperm and the egg, GOD places a spark of light (considered to be the soul) into the conception.

If the pentagram is meant to represent the female, with her five points, versus the males' six points, then again this symbolical representation is perfect when it is realized that every conception first conceives a female and it is not until the introduction of the Y-chromosome that the fetus begins to form into a male.

Next consider that the pentagram is inverted with the fifth point, representing Light, pointing down. In the human, the head, or highest point, is the seat of supreme consciousness. Further, it is in the head, brain or Seventh Sphere where one receives the highest spiritual enlightenment. In the pentagram, this fifth point (white) would also represent the head just as Christ, pictured hanging below the I.N.R.I., is the head of the Church and GOD's kingdom in the Bible. In this light the reader can see the position of the fetus in the womb, with its' body inverted so that its' head is facing downward (just like the Star) and we see the proper position of birth (head first).

With these facts in mind, one would be forced to view the allegory of the crucifixion, and the inverted pentagram which it alludes to, as a further or deeper allusion to the descent of the Godform into physical matter and subsequent birth as a human being.

To support this explanation of the allegory one must consider that in the Christian religion Jesus is worshipped as being THE GOD incarnated into a human body just as the pentagram alludes to the combination of the Elements and Spirit incarnated into a human body.

In Illustration 4-C the reader will see the name of GOD as written by the Jewish people. These written letters are commonly referred to as the *Tetragrammaton* by occult practitioners as well as ritual magicians.

A review of the inef-

Illustration 4-C

fable name of Jehovah (the *Tetragrammaton*) also relates the same theme as the allusion of the pentagram and crucifixion. The letters of the *Tetragrammaton* are written right to left as is all written dialogue in the Hebrew language; however, when the letters are stacked one upon the other they form a pretty good basic form of the Material-Body. Why would this be if it was not meant to be? Can the enlightened reader truly tell himself or herself that the name of the Jewish GOD, when written vertically rather than horizontally, depicts the form of the Material-Body merely by accident or coincidence? Even if this could be believed using only that synchronicity as the deciding factor, what then when one considers the information within the allegory of the crucifixion of Jesus, which alludes to the pentagram, and which itself alludes to the incarnation of GOD into matter?

Need more evidence? Consider the Islamic title for THE GOD: ALLAH. In Illustration 4-D the author has taken those five letters and positioned them around the vertically written *Tetragrammaton*. As positioned in Illustration 4-D, those letters can easily be seen to allude to the five-points of the Material-Body, to wit:

A= Arm
L= Leg
L= Leg
A= Arm
H= Head.

Here again the author is forced to stress the knowledge that ALL religions and belief systems, including atheism, have at their center the very same object in view: MAN (Self).

Included within this concept is the fact that these same belief systems and religions ALL promote the uplifting, betterment or struggle to *be like GOD* or the messiah; that is, for man to aspire to something greater and in those religions, that something greater is *GOD* himself. In those systems it is the ultimate goal of those adhering to those systems to *be like GOD*.

There can be no doubt then that the concept of Lucifer as the enemy, because he caused Adam and Eve to desire to *be like GOD*, is folly because the secret-teachings hidden within the orthodox

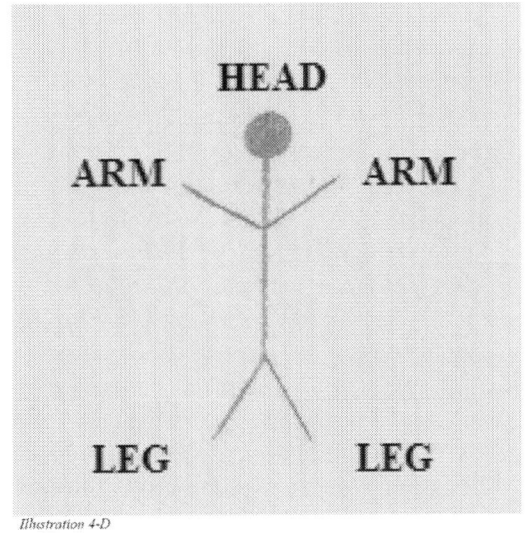

Illustration 4-D

49

religions, which present Lucifer as the 'bad guy', is the core ideology that: (1) man is GOD incarnated into physical matter and the Material-Body; and (2) to return to the status of GOD, man must struggle to *be like GOD* and take part in the esoteric teachings and practices whereby man can transcend the trap of Creation and avoid eternal damnation or death.

Truly, it is only because of the enlightenment and encouragement to '*be like*' GOD, promoted by Lucifer in the allegory, or ideology that character represents, that man has any hope to one day escape imprisonment within the muddy vesture of decay.

With the realization that ALL orthodox religions encompass the secret teachings of the godhood of humanity, the enlightened mind must next begin to actively seek the attainment of supreme consciousness through Self-realization. This is that which occurs during the process outlined in the plethora of Luciferian doctrines and the knowledge of Self was the precursor to becoming "...like [Them]" as outlined in Genesis, 3:22.

Where the descent of the Godform into matter, as man or woman, is a trap and seemingly endless cycle for the un-conscious and un-enlightened mind; so must ascension back into unity with the Godform be the goal and destination of Illuminati. The experience of the material creation is an ensnarement which must be repeated endlessly, for those without eyes to see, until enlightenment dawns within Their mind(s); as such, the Earthly experience must be utilized for the achievement of union, or re-unification, of the 'I' or 'Self' and the Godform. When this happens, then takes place the evolution which raises one from a living-man into a conscious and living-god; or, in other words, from a Son of MAN into a Sun of GOD.

The ancient's spoke of many lives the Godform must experience throughout the eternal span of that living-soul. This experience was said to take place in differing forms and on differing planets and pseudo-Earths. For example, the kabalistic teachings infer that first, earth and water combine to make the stone wherein resides the Godform as, or in, the life of the stone; in the proper time, the Godform leaves the form of a stone and reincarnates into material life, but this time as a plant. Later, and again in the proper time, the Godform leaves the form of a plant to reincarnate into matter as an animal. Next, after the proper amount of time, the Godform enters the form of a human being. Along this same line of reasoning then, it must be perceived that once the Godform has spent the requisite amount of time in the form of man, he must shuck the form of the man and become something wholly different in the same manner as he did previously from stone to plant, plant to animal, and animal to human.

It was considered that the incarnation of that Godform upon this Earth was a unique experience representing the lowest point (descent into matter) of the Godforms evolutionary process and was viewed to be but a dream wherein the un-conscious and un-aware entity slept, all the while being ignorant to his or her true identity. It was that very ignorance which was considered to be the trap of reincarnation into the Material-Body. Despite this viewpoint, incarnation upon this Earth into a Material-Body was simultaneously viewed as the crowning-glory for those who achieved awareness of their true identity; for, in this achievement of self-awareness, lay the key to the promotion and evolution back into the universal or cosmic GODHOOD whereby We, Illuminati, are destined to complete, replenish and govern the inter-dimensional realities of eternity.

It is this crowning-glory that is the envy of all beings whose station is fixed and un-movable. In submitting to the Earthly and material experience, with the chance of remaining trapped for eternity, the Godform which was incarnated into a Material-Body has undertaken a trial of tremendous consequence as well as possible reward.

Through knowledge of the descent of the Godform into the Material-Body, Illuminati may proceed with the evolution of the 'I' into the reptilian consciousness of the Light-Body. We are the so-called Serpent People.

Notice that in Illustration 4-A the author has depicted Jesus on the cross as a black man. It is the author's wish that he could know the thoughts of every single person who just read the preceding sentence. As those words were written, the author literally had the biggest smile on his face and was laughing out loud!

Illuminati, do We understand that We are the Sun and part of an unimaginable whole? Do We understand that the melanin within Our reptilian skin is the key to the absorption of the powers and energies of the GODDESS, known as the universal ether or Light, as well as the absorption of the powers and energies of the GOD by and through his Sun?

The role of Horus/Jesus, along with the right-side-up pentagram, was intentionally assigned to the so-called white-race while Ra/Lucifer, along with the up-side-down pentagram, was intentionally assigned to the so-called black-race. Both are noted to be the Morning Star; however, Lucifer was given the role of the bad and evil morning star while Jesus was given the role of the good and holy morning star. Lucifer was promoted as the originator and father of sin while Jesus was promoted as the savior and redeemer of sin.

In this manner, the black-race was made to be undesirable and redeemable only through the desirable white-race. As the Sons and Daughters of the Pharaohs, the black-race was demoted from the status of living-gods, and rulers of the world, to animal-men through metaphorical execution and the theft of the secrets by which they had previously created a civilized society and sustained their world-empire.

Google the video to the song *Smile*, where Tupac Shakur is depicted as being nailed to the cross and now consider his position in that video, as well as the illustration on the cover of his CD (*Machiavelli: The Seven Day Theory*), in light of this information.

Redemption will ensue when the Sons and Daughters of the Pharaohs actively and openly seek and demand reception of their inheritance. At that time, mankind will be restored and saved through the interplanetary and inter-dimensional co-existence of the Gods and humanity.

Illuminati know and are not affected by the knowledge of these Truths. It is Our ability to rise above the Tree of Knowledge, which inflames the passions and emotions of the unenlightened, that allows Us to partake of the Tree of Life. In order for this to take place We must be able to use this knowledge for the purpose of evolution into the New Age rather than allow it to keep us submersed in the current state or era. The knowledge of history, and the past rule of the Empire, must be viewed and understood in 360°.

With this knowledge comes either enlightenment or blinding emotion. Which one applies to the reader is based on the answer to one simple question: Are you one of Us?

CHAPTER FIVE

A DIFFERENT PAIR OF GLASSES

In a Kabalistic sense, Lucifer knew that Jehovah was in fact NOT the Most High God, but was actually a Secondary Deity, also known as the *mover of the waters* in the book of Genesis as demonstrated in the following verse: "And the earth was without form, and void; and darkness was upon the face of the deep. And the spirit of God moved upon the face of the waters." Genesis 1:2.

It was those *waters* which represents the Primary Deity, the *GODDESS*, in that allegory. There, Jehovah was not inclined to allow mankind *to know* or *be like* them; however, the Serpent WAS inclined to allow mankind to aspire to the same station as Jehovah, and thus, cause mankind to become *like* them.

In the Garden, the Serpent was NOT inclined to allow mankind to remain ignorant of the fact that the humans had been created *in their image*. In that allegory, Jehovah was the Grand Architect, the *macrocosmic* demiurge, and originator of the thought or idea of material creation who himself could never be part of the creation lest his energy and power destroy it all. Lucifer was one part of Jehovah's creative thought, part of a dual-aspect thought emanation, which itself materialized and became the *microcosmic* demiurge causing life to spring forth in the material universe, specifically Earth. As noted, the Grand Architect's emanation had a dual-aspect nature in the same manner that a coin has two sides but is only a single coin. If Lucifer was one side of this coin then obviously, in the Christian sense, Jesus (Christ) was the *flipside* of that *coin*. This dual-aspect emanation is comparative to the Egyptian serpent-myth which was also dual-aspect in nature and was called the Agathodaimon/Kaikodaimon.

The question here is: being only the mover of the waters could the above-described trinity, -Jehovah, Lucifer, Jesus-, have stopped the Adam from becoming aware that the Grand Architect is the Secondary Deity? If all forms of everything that could ever exist were already in existence in those 'waters' could the Grand Architect have prevented the Adam from realizing that he, the Adam, was actually an 'ordered' embodiment of the Most High Goddess (the waters) who represents the Supreme Chaos just as the Grand Architect was an 'ordered' embodiment of Her chaos? Could the meaning of the Latin phrase "ORDO AB CHAO" been concealed from mankind forever? Probably not. Can the meaning of that phrase be any clearer to Us? Once again, probably not.

It must be remembered here that the Grand Architect, Jehovah, was not the creator of life on the Earth; rather, he was the one from whose imagination sprang forth the idea or WORD which is His dual-aspect emanation and the actual creator or placer of life into its material form on Earth. This statement is reinforced by the Christian doctrine where, in the Gospel of John, it is noted: "In the beginning was the Word, and the Word was with God, and the Word was God. The same was in the beginning with God. All things were made by him; and without him was not anything made that was made. In him was life; and the life was the light of men." John 1:1-4.

In all primitive religions, the 'son of the father' is the creative god (i.e., his thought made visible). As stated above, the father is akin to the macrocosmic demiurge; the son, to the dual aspect emanation and microcosmic demiurge.

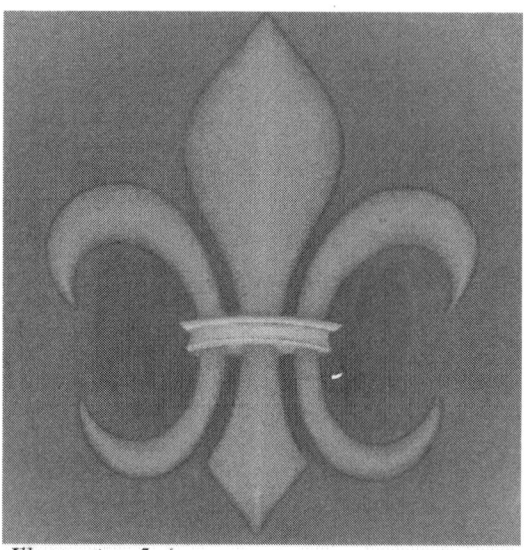

Illustration 5-A

Fleur-de-Lis

Consider here the fleur-de-lis shown in Illustration 5-A. The Secondary Deity (Jehovah) is symbolized by the middle-pillar or flower. The left and right curved pillars, or second and third flowers, symbolize his dual aspect emanation (Jesus/Lucifer), who is the creative emanation or WORD, -known to the Egyptians as Agathodaimon and Kaikodaimon-, who entered material existence as the Sun while the middle-stem (Jehovah) remains unseen. In this manner the fleur-de-lis more accurately depicts the 'Trinity' than does most contemporary religious symbology or explanations.

The allegorical fleur-de-lis described above is only the GOD of the created material universe which maintains a certain 'Order' out of the Primary Deity's 'Chaos' (hence the Latin phrase, Ordo ab Chao). That Primary Deity is the universal female principle, or primeval force, and the true Most High God (Goddess).

While the dictionary defines the fleur-de-lis as "a decorative motif consisting of three Iris flowers", the author presents here that the literal English translation might cause the esoteric student to think otherwise. The translation is literally: "Flower of the Lily".

Anyone who has ever been to a pond or body of water consisting of aquatic botany will recognize that the Lily pad is but a leaf of the Asian Water Lily more commonly known as the Lotus flower. The Lotus is defined as "an Asian Water Lily having large leaves and pinkish flowers". As with most types of flowers, the Lotus is found colored in hues other than this pinkish type. Thus, when the phrase 'flower of the lily' is examined, it might be more commonly envisioned as being a Lotus flower, and lily-pad leaf, than the afore-given definition of an Iris flower. However, the reader may want to consider that the Water Lily was also depicted in ancient Egyptian hieroglyphics surrounding different Gods/Goddesses, particularly Osiris and Isis. Those lilies were not the Lotus type but were nonetheless Water Lilies. In the Egyptian hieroglyphics, one will find a central Water-Lily springing forth from the water in full bloom; likewise, the hieroglyphics contain two lesser Water-Lilies, one on the left side and one on the right, next to the central flower. Either way, it is the water lily that is the perfect symbol of the Secondary Deity, with his dual-aspect emanation, because the picture alludes to the fleur-de-lis springing forth from the water which can only be viewed esoterically as the Secondary Deity springing forth from the primeval waters of the Primary Deity.

It is the author's stance that the meaning, or flower, of the phrase 'fleur-de-lis' is double and cryptic so as to evade detection by all but the sincere occult student for the reasons set forth below. This type of "double-speak", more commonly known as rhetoric, is typical in esoteric and occult studies when dealing with matters, phrases, symbols, and entire documents relative to the era(s) of persecution carried out by the Roman Catholic Church.

Many associate the fleur-de-lis with the historical royal families of France; however, the royal families were simply the latest people to be associated with the Water Lily and, as set forth above by the author, the esoteric symbol itself is but a modern rendition of an age-old Truth explained by means of symbolic allusion.

To find the beginning of the Water Lily's use in religion or occult knowledge, one must delve into the Hindu Vedas where he or she would first find mention of the Lotus flower in the story of Brahma's discovery of Self and his realization that he is resting upon that flower which itself floats upon the waters. The Water Lily is found in the Egyptian teachings, as noted above, and also in Buddhist teachings to depict much the same, that is, the presence of the Divine Feminine and esoteric waters as the Primary Deity while the masculine Creator is viewed as the Secondary Deity. One would also find use of the flower of the lily in Christian symbology, for instance, where the Archangel Gabriel is seen to bestow upon the Virgin Mary a bouquet of Lilies in a famous painting ordained by none other than the Roman Catholic Church.

The Water Lilies must be viewed then as historical and esoteric hand-me-downs revealing the true nature of the Primary Deity, Secondary Deity, and the latters' dual aspect emanation. As is equally obvious from history, the true nature of the fleur-de-lis, as employed in France by the royal families, almost certainly could not have been presented to the Masses lest the royal families, and anyone speaking or possessing such knowledge, be accused of heresy by the Church of Rome. Any persons possessing such knowledge, including members of the clergy, would have necessarily been forced to keep this information secret, only revealing such Truths under the most strict and secret circumstances.

The symbolic Water Lilies find their existence submersed in water just as they are found in Nature. When in bloom, the flower will rise to the surface of the water, spring forth therefrom and open, or bloom. The Lotus flower never actually leaves the water, as its' stem is more of an umbilical cord type apparatus, and thus cannot be said to 'spring' from the water as does other Water Lilies. The Lotus will usually spend a significant portion of that day resting, or floating, upon the surface of the water after it rises to the surface to bloom. After its' blossoming period is over, the Lotus then closes and returns to its' resting place within, or beneath, the water where it resides until such time as it will rise again to the surface of the water to bloom once more.

The author leaves it up to the reader to decide exactly what type of Water Lily is depicted by the fleur-de-lis because, regardless of the specific flower envisioned by the reader, the same occult Truth is being conveyed thereby.

The fleur-de-lis, being a symbolical example of the Secondary Deity and His emanation(s), is an even more perfect representation of Deity when the symbol itself is visualized as floating atop the waters in which it grows; said water representing the Primary Deity both in and from which the flower finds its very life.

It must further be perceived that the Primary Deity is Herself the true parent-source of anything considered to be good as well as evil. The Creator, as normally named and described by orthodox religion, is not the Most High God; He is only the father, and thinker, of matter, which is bad or evil, and spirit, which is good or holy. Both simply emanate from the highest and invisible cause (Her) and pass through Him (Christianity's Jehovah), as though through a vehicle, and then proceed to pervade into the whole universe of created matter as Life through His dual-aspect emanation (Jesus/Lucifer): the Sun.

Tree of Life

When considering the Tree of Life, as found in the Kabbalah, it should first be recognized that there are ten circles connected to each other in a systematic manner by twenty-two lines or paths. An overview of Illustration 5-B will evidence this statement.

These ten circles and twenty-two lines together equal thirty-two. For this reason, Scottish Rite and Prince Hall masonic lodges proffer a system of esoteric teachings consisting of thirty-two levels or degrees. Although these systems have thirty-three levels or degrees, the mystical 33° of Freemasonry is

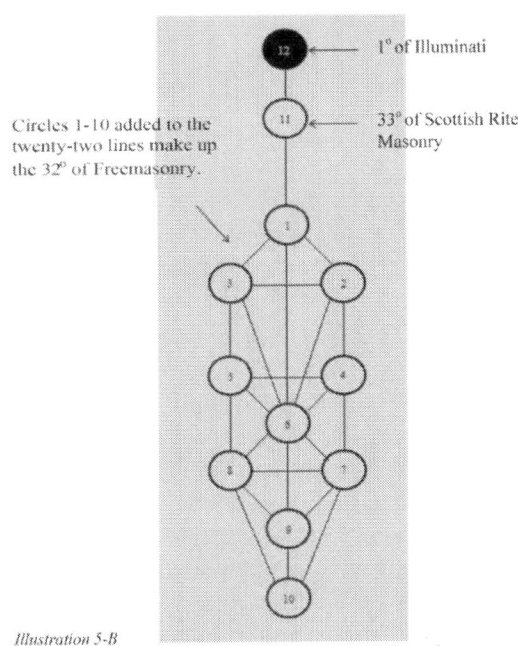

1° of Illuminati

33° of Scottish Rite Masonry

Circles 1-10 added to the twenty-two lines make up the 32° of Freemasonry.

Illustration 5-B

rarely bestowed upon a mason until after the death of his Material-Body.

When considering the Tree of Life then, the 33° would have to be an eleventh circle that resides separate from the interconnected thirty-two degrees and directly above the circle known as Kether or Crown and numbered as 'One' in Illustration 5-B.

The author sets forth that the ten circles and twenty-two lines ("32°") alludes to all matter and life which exists in the created universe, while the eleventh circle ("33°") alludes to the Grand Architect, that Secondary Deity, who must forever remain outside and separated from the created universe lest he destroy all that exists with his brilliant radiance and power. Only his IDEA (Logos) and dual-aspect emanation can exist within the created universe and it is that emanation (Sun) which created all life on Earth.

With the understanding that the 33° alludes to the Secondary Deity, the enlightened mind must consider at which place in the allegorical Tree of Life would the Primary Deity reside or be placed? It would be reasonable as well as logical to deduce that since the 32° system emanates from the 33°, then the 33° must have come forth from the thirty-fourth degree ("34°"). This deduction would be logical in light of the understanding that the Secondary Deity became manifest from the life of the Primary Deity as shown in the allegory depicting the Water Lily springing forth from the primeval waters. As such, the circle representing the 34° would be a twelfth circle residing directly above the circle representing the 33° and would allude to the Black Sun, the Primary Deity.

She is the Black Sun above the Tree of Life and above the 33°. Her brilliance is so intense that it is Her Light which shines upon and permeates ALL, with the exception of NONE. Although the un-enlightened might picture Her as the 34°, this is not so. She is the 1° of Illuminati and this is that so secret of secrets and the conclusion given is: It is Her LIFE which We seek to aspire to and Her LIGHT We hope to re-submerse Ourselves in.

Consider how the planet Venus (Goddess of Love and Fertility) , also known as the Eastern and Morning Star, leads the Sun (God of Life, Death

57

and Re-birth) into glorious splendor each Spring and Summer morning. This cosmic activity is the macrocosm of man and woman's GREAT microcosmic relationship.

In the macrocosm above, Venus is the Goddess while the Sun is God. Likewise, in the microcosm woman must necessarily play the role of the goddess, or Venus, while man must necessarily play the role of god, or Sun.

In the same manner that Venus leads the Sun into cosmic splendor on a daily basis, so the goddess (the incarnation of the Goddess energies) can lead god (the incarnation of the God energies) into glorious splendor; however, just as Venus can also lead the Sun into night, so can Venus lead the Sun into eradication and despair. It is thus necessary that the microcosmic Venus KNOW who and what she is along with the understanding that, like Sirius, she is the TRUE source of the microcosmic Suns' potency. When the enlightened Venus knows that she is the Primary Specimen, the incarnate goddess, and the source of the incarnated Suns' glory, then does she become a conduit for the celestial powers and radiance to enter into that god, her Sun. Likewise, the enlightened Sun will then reflect back unto Venus her own potency which is LIFE itself.

It is only on account of the Goddess that the conscious awakening of the Appointed One has come about; for it was the discovery that he was being watched by Her manifestation, Isis, through the dimensional veil, that set into motion the keys to the puzzle of his incarnation into the Material-Body called James. For this reason, the Appointed One, the Prince of ATUM, is also known to be the Prophet of Isis in the New Age of The Empire.

It is the re-awakening of mankind to the presence and existence of the GODDESS that must be achieved in order that the Earth's frequencies can be returned to a state which is compatible with the frequencies governing the multi-dimensional universe. Until She is globally acknowledged Earth will be prohibited from returning to its proper place in the multi-verse.

CHAPTER SIX

IRONY OF THE AMERICAN ERA

*"We have to talk about liberating the minds
as well as liberating society."*

-Angela Davis

The irony mentioned here is the historical use of religion to conquer, enslave, and brainwash an entire portion of the United States' population, namely the African-American community. Of course, this took place long after the same religion was used to mentally enslave the Europeans themselves although the enslavement of these people took place so long ago that it is rather difficult to examine the process without going into a lengthy study and discussion that mostly is not pertinent to this manuscript.

In the days of early European colonialism, native tribes within the African continent would systematically capture members of rival tribes and sell them into slavery. These captives would be taken by their European purchasers to the island of Haiti where the slaves would be auctioned off and transported to other areas of the world. Once in the new destination, the slaves would then be resold for profit to individuals who would become their legal owners. One such hub, offering the trade, sale or purchase of human beings was none other than the United States of America. This is historical fact.

After the purchase of a slave, the supposed owner of that person would normally have taken measures to ensure that the transition into slavery was complete in order to prevent rebellion, escape, and most likely, violence which could have easily been bestowed upon the so-called masters by the slave population. The process used to ensure that a slave's transition into slavery was complete was nothing more or less than a form of psychological warfare which the average slave was not fully equipped to defend against. The process of completion was carried out mostly because the slave population of the average plantation far outnumbered the number of slavers; however, some of the so-called masters were simply psychopathic brutes who found in their slaves the easiest prey and outlet for their dark and violent predispositions. Thus, conditioning, brainwashing, fear and division amongst slaves were key elements in the strategy of maintaining order and control over the slave populations of the plantations.

Other than the whip, death and fear of being separated from family, religion (specifically the doctrine of Jehovah and belief in Jesus Christ as lord and savior) was the most powerful tool employed by the slave owners in their strategy to maintain control. The African slaves were systematically subjected to the doctrine of Jehovah, which was interpreted by their American captors in a manner so as to ensure widespread brainwashing and conditioning of the slave in order to bring about the attitude of acceptance of his or her position as a slave. The conditioning and brainwashing created by the Christian religion was so complete that after only one or two generations, the brainwashed slaves began to assume the role once played by the captors; that is, the slaves began to teach the captors' interpretations of the Book to their own descendants and fellow slaves and so, began to ensure the complete acceptance of their condition without the slave owners having to continue performing this task themselves.

The author takes time here to note that most likely the slaves initially began to assume identity with, and belief in, the doctrine of Jehovah solely under the disguised purpose of self-preservation. It would only be fair to the slave to point out here that, while not believing the lies of the white-man's religion, the slaves were mostly smart enough to know that if they at least appeared to believe, their lives and conditions would be better than if they openly opposed the doctrine. Equally obvious, is that these intelligent persons did not desire for their offspring to be tortured, beaten or experience the harsher physical living conditions they no doubt witnessed and experienced time and time again. With the memories of death and pain at the hands of the enforcers firmly in mind, the slaves no doubt began to teach the doctrine of Jehovah to their own children, grandchildren and other slaves new to the plantation.

Most likely these 'teachers' would not let their descendants know that their belief in, and acceptance of, the white-man's religion was a method employed solely for the benefit of avoiding the brutality of the slave-master(s); to do so, might prevent those descendants from accepting their conditions in life and might lead to uprisings at the cost of many additional lives. Eventually, the Christian religion was whole-heartedly accepted by the slaves, along with their position as property, due to the fact that the real reason for the initial acceptance of the doctrine was gradually forgotten by them. At some point it was forgotten altogether that the religion was used by the slave owners as a tool to enslave not only the body of the African, but the mind as well.

The author here asks the reader, "What slavery is more complete, enslavement of the body or enslavement of the mind?" Enslavement of the mind leads to the loss of consciousness.

Today, in 2018, in the United States of America, an overwhelming majority of African-Americans identify themselves as Christians. Almost none of these persons EVER consider that it was the identification with the Christian religion that solidified their enslavement one hundred and fifty-two years ago and, most definitely, NONE who identify as Christians will consider these facts objectively because they are still subjected to the same mental boundaries created during that era. At best, consciousness has been contained and bound; at worst, it has been lost altogether.

The author sets forth that Jehovah and Jesus are foreign deities to the land of Africa despite the fact that today, after much European colonialism on that continent, many Africans consider themselves to be Christians.

The Africans brought to America through the slave trade were NOT Christians of their own free will and accord; rather, the religion was a tool employed to bring harm, pain and death to both their minds and bodies. The slaves did not come to America as Christians and the Christian religion was not an avenue with which they were familiar or which they chose to travel of their own accord.

How many Americans today, African-Americans and otherwise, are still bound by the chains and slavery of the Christian doctrine of Jehovah. Only enlightenment and the Liberation of Self through the Doctrine(s) of Lucifer can bring about freedom of body, mind, and spirit.

The irony today is the acceptance of Jehovah and Jesus by the African-American population as their GOD and Savior, respectively, when in reality the doctrine of Jehovah and Jesus was their SATAN (adversary) and Enslaver, rather than Savior. When slavery was outlawed, and segregation ended, the resulting condition of American society, African-Americans included, was the liberation of society without the liberation of society's mind.

WAKE UP PEOPLE

CHAPTER SEVEN

WHO WE ARE

*"Instantly a light as of a thousand suns
shone down from above me,
And pierced and broke into fragments the
dark cloud which enveloped America."*

-George Washington
Copy of reprint of
National Tribune, Vol. 4, No. 12,
December 1880

The author would here take the time to credit fellow author Stewart Swerdlow, writer of several books, including an interesting read entitled *Blue Blood. True Blood: Conflict and Creation.*

It was a portion of that book, namely pages 201, 202 and 203 which provided the author here with the concept of this particular portion of this chapter. Although Swerdlow's material is not listed here verbatim, so as to constitute plagiarism, a portion of his above-listed book did act as a foundation for the following seventeen paragraphs. The author recommends the purchase and reading of the afore-named book by Swerdlow. It is the author's belief and opinion that Swerdlow's book contains within the text certain key words and/or phrases that may act as triggers which might cause those whose consciousness is evolved to become consciously aware of WHO and WHAT they really are. Those triggers might activate any prior preparation and evolution, which took place in the last age, in those individuals whose 'I-consciousness' and 'Self-consciousness' was evolved in that particular era but who have, up to this point, identified with the Ego in this era rather than with the Godform.

Perception is everything. In a certain way, perception is GOD and the ability to perceive, consciously, is what makes Us 'living-gods' and Illuminati. In line with this statement is also the concept that each individual person, or persona, along with each individual thing encountered, is simply a reflection of your very own perception. Or, in other words, as Swerdlow believes, it is all a reflection of your own though-pattern(s). Think of it this way, the author can interact with Jane Doe and perceive her in whatever way he perceives Her. The reader, while witnessing the exact same interaction, between Jane Doe and the author, at the same exact time, can walk away with a completely different perception of Her than the author's perception. These differing perceptions are nothing more than two differing reflections;

one reflected onto Jane Doe by the author, the other reflected onto Her by the reader. However, which is the true perception? Or, are the two differing perceptions each equally true if it is considered that the author and reader both represent a separate and distinct universe where individual perception is the GOD of both?

If this can be fathomed as Truth, then We, Illuminati, are also only reflections of other people's perceptions as well as Our own. Thus, if after reading Chapter One, the reader found that he or she is not one of the Enlightened Ones, then it is that very perception of what he or she is not that makes Our existence as Illuminati valid. It makes Us what we are.

If the reader does not consider himself or herself an Enlightened One, should Illuminati be feared and considered evil then? The author sets forth that the answer is NO, because Our existence as such is simply a reflection of ones' own perception and thought patterns. And if that be so, what can the reader learn from his or her own thought-patterns by studying, reflecting and perceiving Us.

An overwhelming majority of the unconscious Masses are oblivious to the fact that We exist. If the reader becomes, or already is, conscious and aware of Our existence then They should be congratulated, for it means They are learning about Themselves and Their own thought-patterns. To reflect Us as Illuminati means they are able to perceive the next step in the esoteric evolutionary process of sublimation.

Should the reader(s) who does not consider Themselves to be one of the Enlightened Ones hate, fear or battle against Us? No. Illuminati believe that We have the right to direct the course of humanity, and We do. It can also be stated that Our belief in Our right to rule also stems from the thought-patterns of the Masses because They believe that We believe in this right. Therefore, it exists and is acknowledged not only by Us, but by Them also. If the reader has perceived that he or she is not Illuminati and does not have the right to direct the course of humanity, then They are not and do not.

Our thought-patterns, as Enlightened Ones, are a natural part of who and what We are. We reinforce Our thought-patterns with other like-minded thought-patterns every minute, every hour and every day that We live and breathe. Think about what this means. As Illuminati, We reflect Our existence onto those We encounter whether They are of conscious mind or not; whether they be fellow Enlightened Ones or not and They, in turn, reflect these patterns right back, giving them life and validity. This is what the unenlightened must learn about his or her thought-patterns, reflections and perceptions.

One will know that they have successfully altered their own thought-patterns when the reflections change; likewise, it is a necessary requirement that the reflection change if the thought-pattern(s) are to be considered changed. If the reflection does not change, then the thought-pattern(s) have not changed. When these thought-patterns change, then the reflection and perception of Us will no longer be the perception of Us being a threat to Them.

We know who We are. We know the Godform and the true identity of Our being. We know that Our true identity lay beneath the assumed identity and persona of the human being and Ego. We choose to identify with the Godform and assume identity as this being, thereby forsaking Our human identity as created by the physical and material brain or mind. We are Illuminati.

If the reader does not consider himself or herself to be an Enlightened One, has the reader ever taken time to consider what the differences between himself or herself and Illuminati are? Listed below are the main differences between the thought-patterns of the Masses and Enlightened Ones:

- We do not possess a victim mentality. Illuminati view Ourselves as being unstoppable by anyone as well as being invincible. Rather than having a victim mentality, We possess the mentality of a winner; leaving no question within Our minds that We will win at whatever We set out to do even where winning might take years. The careful layout of Our plans, whether they are personal or global, is then strategically carried out in order to bring about Our purpose and desire.

- We do not have an inferiority complex and We do not feel less than, or beneath, anyone. Illuminati know that We are superior to the unconscious Masses and there exists no doubt whatsoever within Our thought-patterns about how great We are. Our superiority is one of the many reasons some of Us elect to be segregated from common society and seldom interact with others outside Our circle(s). Illuminati are not myopic in any way and view the world as Ours.

- We do not have low self-worth issues and there is no one who can make Us feel bad about Ourselves or unworthy of anything. Contrary to low self-worth, Illuminati have tremendously high levels of self-worth and not only do Our friends and family reinforce these beliefs but so does the media, entertainment industry and the average citizen We might encounter. Everywhere We go people honor Us and desire to be included in Our lives in some form or fashion, no matter how minute.

- We do not have guilt issues and Illuminati believe that We are justified in all that We do. We are not burdened by the conscience as are those of the Masses because We are no longer ensnared by the Tree of Knowledge. Since We are not predisposed to feelings of guilt for the actions We take, We have no doubt that We deserve the very best that physical reality has to offer.

- We do not have issues of lack and Illuminati know that We not only have the time and resources for whatever it is We need but

We also are consciously aware of the powers, energies and forces of the universe that are at Our disposal if and when We so choose to utilize them. As such, Illuminati know that We currently possess secret knowledge. We can access these abilities and knowledge at any time as well as determine what knowledge will be revealed to the Masses.

- We do not live in denial. Illuminati know who and what We are and We are proud of it. We have no desire to be in the evolutionary condition of the Masses. We know that We are reptilian beings of Light in possession of the DNA of the Gods. Illuminati do not deny that the conscious awareness of Our Godform makes us a whole different species than those of the Masses. We live in a dual-reality existence rather than in denial; for to deny the existence of an inter-dimensional or a dual-reality would be an act causing Us to revert to being a member of the Masses. This form of denial is all but impossible for Us. We know Our purpose and Illuminati do not have to search to know that Our purpose is to prepare and condition society to accept and desire to share planet Earth with the Gods. There is no doubt in the mind of Illuminati what We are here to do.

- We do not place limitations on Ourselves and Illuminati believe We are limitless. We do not believe in limitations to Our power, Our power to influence others, including society, or Our ability to bring about Our personal and collective desires.

Now that the most pointed differences in the basic self-identity and characteristics of Us and Them are so clearly set forth, it is easy to see why We are what We are and there can be no doubt of Our identity. We are the very Ones who shall rule the New World Order on behalf of the Gods.

We are now at the point where We can scientifically bring about the matter-less Earth and finally rid the Godform of the Material-Body. Through the science of chemicals, the Matrix is available to those who can operate using the perspective of the Light-Body; that is, the reptile consciousness.

The evolution of the Light-Body and the attainment of the reptilian psyche or consciousness, while at the same time finally shedding the skin of matter, can be achieved even by those who might normally be considered to be weak or beginners in this process. The pharmacy (certain natural as well as man-made chemicals) has been prepared to allow for the enhancement of the reptilian consciousness while evolving from one demanding form (physical) into the next (ethereal); in short, from Material to Light.

The attainment of the reptile consciousness is of utmost importance to the development of the Light-Body. Only when We become aware of Our true Self, as the reptile or serpent, will We be able to consciously begin to work towards and create the evolution of the Light-Body. In the same manner which We currently experience the material world through the Material-

Body's eyes, so must We allow the Serpent to see through the 'Third-Eye'. A review of Illustration 7-A will highlight the form of the Serpent as seen from a frontal viewpoint and without the physical body blocking or preventing this view.

Just as the planet Saturn rules and governs the Sixth Sphere of the Light-Body ('Third-Eye') so will that planet govern the evolution of that Sphere because it is the evolution of the 'Third-Eye' that is the prerequisite to life in the New Age of the Reptilian Empire.

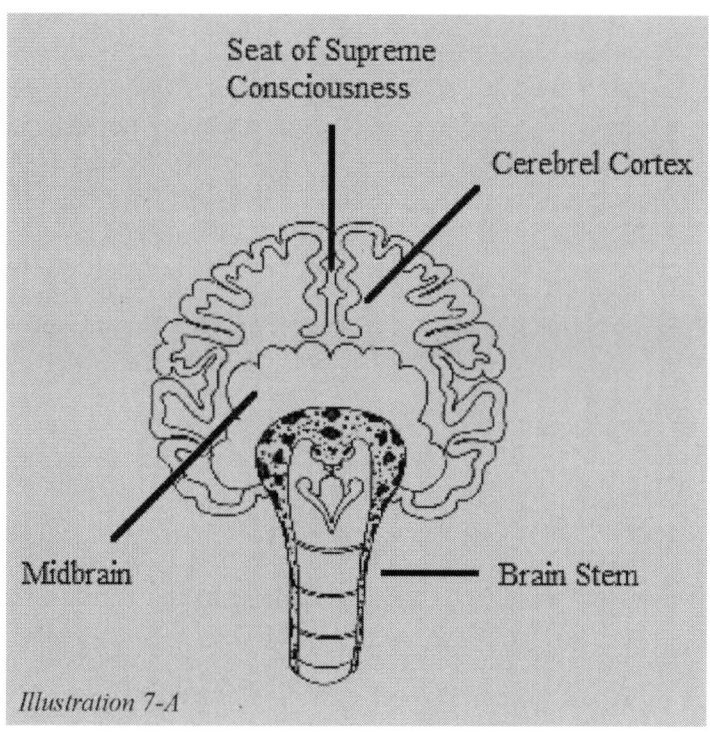

Illustration 7-A

CHAPTER EIGHT

THE GODS OF EGYPT

The Original Nine

Geb-	God of the Earth
Isis/Aset-	Universal Goddess, Great Goddess of the Moon
Ra/Khepri-	Patron Deity of Egypt, God of the Sun, God of Laws and Kingship
Nepthys-	Protector of Children and Comforter in the Afterlife, Wife of Set and Mother of Anubis
Nut/Nuit-	Goddess of Night and the Starry Heavens
Osiris-	Ruler of the Underworld, Lord of Life, Death and Rebirth, Husband of Isis, Father and Brother of Horus
Set/Seth-	God of Chaos, Storms, Darkness, Violence, the Uncreated universe and Burning Red Desert * Antithesis of Ma'at and nemesis of Osiris/Horus
Shu-	God of Hot Dry Winds, the Atmosphere and Breath of Life, God of the Fire Element. * Holds apart the heavens (Nut) and Earth (Geb)
Tefnut-	Goddess of Cool and Moist Afternoon Breezes as well as Gentle Rains, Goddess of the Water Element

Allegory of Creation

Ra, the Sun God, united with His own shadow to beget Shu (dry air) and Tefnut (rain clouds). These two then united, bringing forth Nut (the heavens) and Geb (the earth). They were held apart by Shu during the day while Ra journeyed across the sky; but at night, Nut descended to rest upon the body of Geb. They became the parents of Isis and Osiris, Set and Nepthys, thus completing 'The Nine' (Ennead) which is the basic pantheon recognized in every temple of Egypt.

The Nine are the governing principles and creators of the created universe that rule and govern ALL life. Together, the Nine make One and there is no other GOD of physical matter than the One the Nine together is: The ATUM.

CHAPTER NINE

REVELATION OF ILLUMINATI

"Who dares think one thing and another tell,
My heart detests him as the gates of Hell."

-POPE

The obvious question presents itself here, "How can We bring the New Age, along with the Doctrine of Light (Self-Liberation from religion), into the arena currently understood to be mainstream?" Next question: "How do We know that the Masses will accept Our doctrine of Synarchy when it is offered to Them?"

The glory of the Truth is that Our answers to the questions above are the very responses They already want to hear, and have been waiting to hear for decades now. Therefore it is those very expectations that We must now provide Them with.

America, the Great Harlot who caused the entire world to be drunk, along with the world at large, is presently standing on the proverbial 'cusp' of evolution into a New Age. The foundation for society's acceptance of the Doctrine of Lucifer has previously been founded and laid thick by the use of the music industry, namely Hip-Hop, Rap, Pop, and R. & B. Even now, the country music being played over the airwaves has begun to take on and reflect the ideologies, vocabulary and overall tone of those music genres; thereby effectively helping to blur the lines between one genre and the next as well as unite the young people of the differing demographics relative to each genre.

Over the last fifty years of the twentieth century, and the first two decades of the twenty-first, the Masses have been fed information concerning Us and the Gods in a manner which has acclimatized Them to the ideas set forth herein. This information has placed Us in a more pleasing light than at any other time in history. It is common today for men, women and children to be familiar with the term Illuminati and to view or consider Us with benevolence rather than the hostility of the ages past. Those familiar and captivated by Our existence range from the early ages of childhood (think seven, eight or nine) to grown adults.

The current mass-preparation of society for evolution into the New Age of the Reptilian Empire has been a longstanding and on-going process for, at minimum, seventy-five years or better. More pointedly, the generations at hand, consisting of roughly those persons forty-five years of age and younger, have realized the need to shed the old skin of orthodox religion(s) in order that the new skin of true spirituality can emerge in full fruition as the science of who and what the so-called human race really is. Likewise, at no other time has the belief and acceptance of extraterrestrial life, i.e. the Gods, been as prominent in the minds of the world's citizens as it is today.

The Age, or time frame, in which We immediately find Ourselves, has come about through certain individual free-thinkers who, during their own lifetimes and eras, found themselves unable to conform to the generally accepted authorities or the religious dogma of those times. It can be asserted that the United States of America was founded precisely upon that particular sentiment which amounted to the people's inability to conform to the British Monarch or Catholic Church's authority. It was the presence of free-thinkers who brought about social evolution in their respective era(s).

Our current Age has been prepared by those such as Eliphas Levi, George Washington, Abraham Lincoln, Dr. Martin Luther King, Jr., Aleister Crowely, Helena Petrovna Blavatsky, Albert Pike, Manly P. Hall, Yusuf Ali, Gerald Gardner, Patricia Crowther, Rudolph Steiner, Raymond Buckland, Alice Baily, Adam Weishaupt, Joel Olsteen and many others not named here but who are equally responsible for preparing the Masses for the institution of the New Reptilian Empire. Likewise, many so-called 'secret-societies' have also played tremendous roles in this preparation.

In accordance with the idea of the preparation for the New Age, and while quoting Professor Josiah P. Cooke, of Harvard University, Madame Blavatsky explicitly sets forth:

> *"[e]very thing in this world has its time[;] and truth... will not root or grow, unless, like a plant, it is thrown into soil in its proper season. The age must be prepared..."*

-Helena Petrovna Blavatsky
Isis Unveiled, Vol. I
p. 146
Wilder Publications 2007

THE AGE HAS BEEN PREPARED; OUR TIME IS NOW.

Together with the afore-named music genres, the public has been familiarized and saturated with the Doctrine of Light through social-media, television, Hollywood and other forms of mass-entertainment and social focus and concentration. These outlets, en banc, have played the role of de-sensitizing the minds, intellects and consciousness's of the American, as well as world, communities. The Masses have been allowed to begin to focus on Self-interests rather than man-made concepts such as religion and service to Jehovah. This focus on Self has helped to prepare Them for the acceptance of the doctrine that teaches that We, and They, are able to attain the Godform through occult practice. Further, this focus on Self rather than religion has allowed for the realization that spiritual enlightenment is obtained through the evolution of Self and the 'I' by focusing on Self rather than a man-made concept of deity.

As an example of the author's assertion of the saturation of the Masses with knowledge of Our presence, the author points out that while this book is being written, television is advertising shows, even wrestling, which openly use the name Lucifer as the main character, use the symbol of the All-Seeing Eye, depict covens of witches, depict users of magic, and depicts all other sorts of occult symbology. Another example of this acclimatization of the Masses to accept the concepts of the New World Order is as follows: at 10:32 in the morning on Thursday, February 23, 2017, while listening to public FM radio, the author briefly heard the phrase "May the God of Your choice..." This phrase, being on free public radio, lends evidence to the author's assessment that the Masses are prepared to denounce orthodox religion and adopt the deification of Self or whatever GOD one might choose to follow along Their chosen Path. It lends evidence that the Masses have accepted that the particular GOD chosen by any individual is not necessarily THE ONLY GOD and the next individual may have a totally different understanding of, and name for, GOD that is equally just as legitimate as the next persons. These individuals would be able to further understand that both of their understandings concerning deity are correct and neither is wrong.

Other examples of the esoteric symbology of the New Age being impressed upon the minds of the public include commercials. For example, there are currently two well-known fast-food restaurants whose advertisements either depict or verbalize the numbers 444.

As seen in the Wendy's commercial they are offering the "444" meal-deal. This particular commercial explicitly uses this number in the advertisement and the numbers can be seen quite clearly in the background.

In a Jack in the Box commercial the company there offers a "Four-For-Four" meal deal. This commercial is probably prohibited from using the explicit numbers 444, as is depicted in the Wendy's commercial, because of some sort of copyright prohibition but the obvious is there for those with eyes to see and ears to hear.

The author's friend has told him on several occasions that "the signs and symbols are for the conscious mind." Thanks for the reminder Washington.

In keeping with the overall idea that the signs of the New Age are making themselves known to the Masses, the author presents the fact that there exists presently a video featuring singer Beyoncé wherein a man and woman's hands are shown resting upon one another. One can only assume, or determine, that those hands belong to none other than Mr. and Mrs. Sean Carter, also known as Jay-Z and Beyoncé, respectively. Upon each of the hands a tattoo of the Roman numeral IV can be clearly identified.

As the author will express shortly, it is his intention to cause Mr. and Mrs. Carter, Jay-z and Beyoncé, to become the Emperor and Empress of Illuminati and the New Age. As such, no man or woman alive would be above them. It is only proper that the three key figures of Illuminati and the New Age of the Reptilian Empire together represent the numerals 444 (IV-IV-IV).

In accord with the number of the Age, 444, the author sets forth that he is the third IV to be added to Mr. and Mrs. Carter's first and second, thus completing the Trinity of Illumination.

With Their focus on Self, rather than a man-made deity, the Masses can focus on, and tread, the Path of Enlightenment with great ease; for They are no longer being bombarded with the doctrine that was created to keep them in Darkness. In short, They can focus on Light and begin to build the Temple. All that would be required of Them now is to begin to practice and exercise the tenets of whichever of the Luciferian Doctrine(s) They personally choose.

> "The [Masses are likened to] a docile and pious child, [who] readily goes wither the nurse leads it. It chooses its idols and fetishes, and worships them in proportion to the noise they make; and then turns round with a timid look of adulation to see whether the nurse, old Mrs. Public Opinion, is satisfied."
>
> -Helena Petrovna Blavatsky
> *Isis Unveiled*, Vol. I
> p. 111-112
> Wilder Publications 2007

We may now enter the world-scene openly by way of the accepted and implicitly deified Hip-Hop, Pop, New Country, Neo-Rock and Hollywood culture, thereby presenting the Masses with the Doctrine of Lucifer which They are already somewhat aware of and which They are already mostly living out in Their day to day lives. Although They are mostly living out the Doctrine of Lucifer in Their daily lives, many are doing so unconsciously. We can do exactly what the Serpent did in the allegory of Eden; We present Jehovah's folly to Them, unabashedly, and depending on their free-will choice, They shall become liberated from the bondage of religion. Just as evolution occurred in the allegory of Eden, the next evolution of creation must take place once again through Self-Knowledge. Again, just like in Eden, the next evolution of creation must take place through a free-will choice rather than through a compelling or forceful source. Their free-will choice will allow Them to understand that once the Doctrine of Light is chosen, there is no going back, so to speak, and so, They must embrace the Light completely if They have any hope at all. With Their free will choice made in favor of Light (when it is made consciously versus the way it is now, unconsciously), They shall realize that They can expect no redemption through Jehovah. Any attempt of redemption through Jehovah would be a step backwards into darkness and to once again truly believe in the lies of religion, once They have experienced Light, would be almost impossible. Point blank. So it will then be up to Them to evolve the Light-Body to a point where They can transfer consciousness into that body in order to exist within It rather than the Material-Body.

When given the opportunity to deny Jehovah and embrace the Doctrine of Lucifer (without facing social retribution) They will do so with great abandon, for mostly, in Their hearts, They have already done so. Now They must do the same with Their mind and will. Jehovah's doctrine demands that They deny Self, while on the other hand, all of the Luciferian Doctrines provide for the illumination, empowerment and indulgence of Self which is exactly what the Masses are truly seeking this very moment.

Presently, like at no other time in our modern history, the stars and celebrities created by the genres listed previously are looked to for guidance in all areas of life by the Masses. Whether this guidance takes form as fashion, food, language, faith, what cars to drive, what clubs to visit, sexuality or what consumables to purchase, said celebrities hold a firm sway over the Masses.

The new-breed is already in place within the younger generations of the U.S. This new-breed consists of those who eagerly await the day that the government will freely hand out monetary credits and other necessities of life in exchange for the acknowledgement of that governing systems entitlement to rule Them. They will anxiously await the allotment(s) provided to them by The Empire. They see true freedom, true prosperity and true equality as acquirements to be gained from a social order unlike the system currently in place. It is the Synarchy of the New Age which They seek.

The music, as well as Hollywood, has brought to Us the generation that will openly uplift Our All-Seeing Eye and openly embrace Illuminati as well as the Reptilian agenda.

"How so?" you ask. Let the author explain in his own voice...

The Appointed One Speaks

> *"Every great dream begins with a dreamer.*
> *Always remember, you have within you the*
> *strength, the patience and the passion to*
> *reach for the stars to change the world."*
>
> -Harriet Tubman

"As the Prince of ATUM, it is my first decree that the recognized face of

Illuminati be altered. Let Illuminati be recognized by the Masses in the faces of those worshipped by Them already (i.e., Drake, Jay-Z, Beyoncé, Bruno Mars, Rhianna, Kanye West, Kim Kardashian, Lil' Wayne, Nicki Minaj, The Weekend, Selena Gomez, Justin Bieber, Taylor Swift, Katy Perry, Arianna Grande, Barack Obama, Michelle Obama, Sandra Bullock, Tom Cruise, Denzel Washington, Sophia Vegara, Will Smith, Jada Pinkett Smith, etc.)

By altering the face of Illuminati I would provide the link of adoration (love) that must exist between the Masses and Enlightened Ones. Further, by this alteration I would provide the eradication of the 'middle-class', leaving only Them and Us. In order that We might fully recognize Our desired end, a one-world order, it is crucial that the link of adoration be allowed to exist between Them and Us by and through the explicit means of Truth closely followed by Their free-will choice and the deification of Their idols.

The benefits gained by the named celebrities, upon gaining status into the fold of Illuminati, will be obvious once the below noted criteria is carried out with great pomp and circumstance.

I will reorganize and raise the Egyptian Pantheon of Nine (the Ennead); thereby causing specific celebrities to assume the Godforms of the ancient Egyptian dynasty. The celebrities shall embody the personalities, personifications and authorities of the Egyptian Gods and Goddesses along with High Priests and Priestesses who will be associated with each God or Goddess. I will also install a Pharaoh (Emperor) to act as a human figurehead of the Ennead's rule.

In this manner, a more definite recognition of the Grand Architect, the 'One from Nine', will be achieved; thereby allowing the proverbial apex stone of the Great Seal to finally be set in order to allow the Empire's full strength in the inauguration of the New Order of the Age, the Reptilian Empire.

Managed correctly, the celebrities shall literally be indwelt by the entity chosen for each of them through ritualistic magical-rites and will thereby literally become the Gods and Goddesses worshipped by the Masses. Although the Masses are almost entirely unaware of it, this is actually already the case. What I propose is simply a conscious awakening of this fact in the minds of the Masses. All that needs to take place is for those celebrities to agree to my proposal and for them to allow the entity hidden within their DNA codes to 'take over' thereby causing or allowing themselves to become that entity, the Godform. Assuming those celebrities are inclined to become Illuminati, allowing the Masses to worship them as Gods and Goddesses, I believe the celebrities will no doubt find this arrangement to be immensely agreeable.

Illuminati and the Universal Doctrine of Light must then perpetually promote said celebrities as the embodiment of the indwelt Gods and Goddesses and in return for life as Gods, the celebrities must perpetually promote Illuminati and the Doctrine of Lucifer. Think cloning, bioengineering, and animatronics. This transformation can take place immediately and We need not wait ages to bring about that which can happen instantly in an almost revolutionary style. This raising of the Egyptian Pantheon is simply 'good-business' and in no way illegal. Refer to the contents of Illustration 9-A and 9-B as examples of this Pantheon.

Just as the Masses spend untold millions of dollars, or other currency, every year to see, hear, or visit Their favorite celebrities, so will They readily flock to worship, deify and spend time with, or around, the newly minted Gods and Goddesses of The Empire."

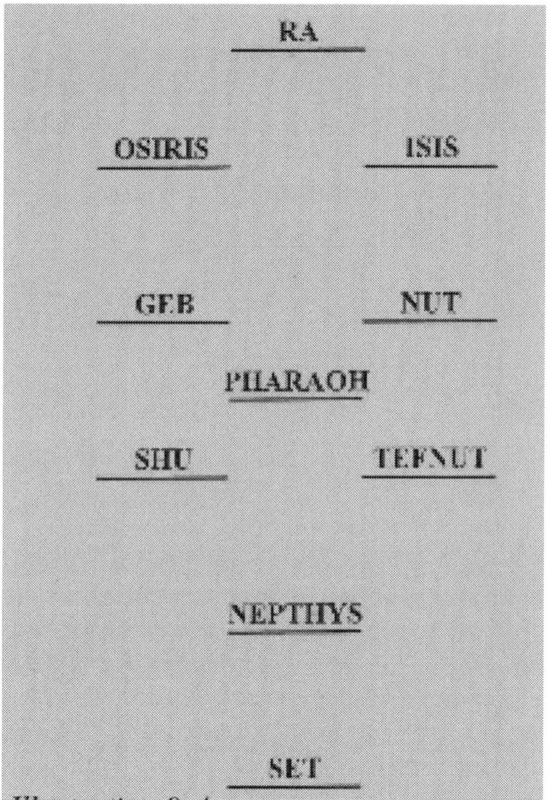

RA

OSIRIS   ISIS

GEB   NUT

PHARAOH

SHU   TEFNUT

NEPHTHYS

SET

Illustration 9-A

Upon the realization of the deification of those celebrities, Our agenda, through Self-Liberation of the Masses, will then have progressed exponentially closer to its' ultimate potential, for We will have secured the web, or link, between religion, state, and entertainment. As such, the Synarchy of Illuminati will be in full control of the three biggest arenas of any one-person's life: the religious, economic and entertainment spectrums. Welcome, The Empire, openly and in full view of the world.

Once it has been made perfectly clear to the Masses that said celebrities are *high-members* of Illuminati, We allow the newly-minted Gods and Goddesses to openly pronounce their Godform to the Masses. As mentioned above, the Masses, as they exist today, are mostly inspired and thrilled with the very idea that We exist. To know that Their favorite celebrities are members of Illuminati will be the publicity needed to incur the acceptance of the Masses and cause Them to desire The Empire. We then further deify those certain celebrities after considerable promotion through free and public ceremonies as well as magical-rites. We make the public a part of it, offering Them direct connection to, and participation in, the ceremonies. Next, the attendants of the ceremonies will be caused to bow in worship to Their newly minted God or Goddess. At this time, the Prince of ATUM, the Appointed

One, shall enter the world-scene and offer the Masses intimate connection to Their chosen God or Goddess by offering Them the opportunity to be microchipped, thereby designating each person microchipped as a member of the Temple in which his or her God or Goddess resides.

"They will openly choose the rule and lifestyle of Illuminati if the decision be presented to Them in the afore-described manner. In this way, Illuminati will gain power OVER the Masses by utilizing the power OF the Masses. (Yes, I'm sick with it.)

The process described above will be further controlled by the creation of The Illuminati Records, L.L.C., a record label which would seek to combine all major artists under this one title. All artists combined under The Illuminati Records, L.L.C. would then either have their individualities dissolved into The Illuminati Records, L.L.C. and/or become subsidiaries of the same. These artists shall become, if not Gods or Goddesses, High Priests and Priestesses of the temples of the Great Ennead which will be strategically positioned around the globe.

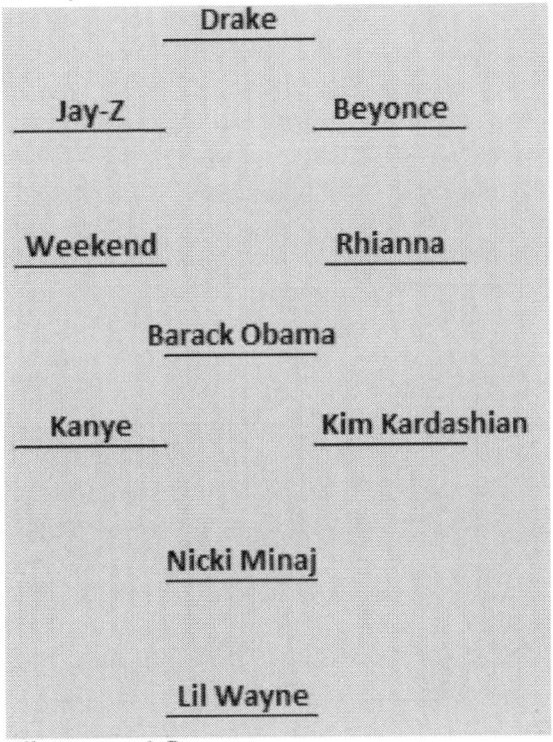

Drake	
Jay-Z	**Beyonce**
Weekend	**Rhianna**
	Barack Obama
Kanye	**Kim Kardashian**
	Nicki Minaj
	Lil Wayne

Illustration 9-B

Artists, think about it, by uniting within the fold of Illuminati We can control the flow of wealth that is produced not only by the record-industry, but also the wealth produced by the advertising market, entertainment market and social-media markets. The way it is now, you are divided and split. Thus, there is not much incentive to help or promote the career of the next person. Divided you fall and remain in the position currently bestowed upon you. United, We can rule the world as Illuminati.

The existing contracts of the afore-mentioned celebrities must be dissolved and/or renegotiated under The Illuminati Records, L.L.C. due to the fact that the Pantheon, as described in Illustrations 9-A and 9-B, including the Temples of each deity, would be subsidiaries of The Illuminati Records, L.L.L."

These maneuvers would essentially and effectively transfer total control of, and power over, mainstream music and entertainment to Illuminati along with an endless supply of wealth, not to mention the overwhelming power of advancement of the Universal Doctrine of Lucifer."

In 1919 the Anglo-American mystic, Alice A. Baily made psychic contact with one of the Hidden Masters, a Tibetan called Djwahal Khul. The Tibetan's teachings centered on the coming of the New Age and the preparation of humanity for that Age. According to the Tibetan, this preparation takes place in three distinct phases: (1) between 1875 and 1890, which was activated through Madame Blavatsky; (2) between 1919 and 1949 through contact with Baily; and (3) the final phase was to begin in 1975 and last until 2025. According to the Tibetan, early on in the twenty-first century a great initiate, the World Teacher, is to appear. Also according to Baily and the Tibetan, revelations from the Hidden Masters and the Hierarchy, after 1975, would be transmitted to the world through the medium of radio.

Basically, the power-move taking place by these actions is that Illuminati would single-handedly be given power and control of the music that plays not only a hugely significant role in the overall psyche of the U.S. population but also the world at large. American Hip-Hop and Pop culture has great influence in regions of the world where alliance with current national leaders is desired, such as, but not limited to, the European Union, United Kingdom, Japan, Russia, China, Australia, Korea (both South and North), South and Central American countries, as well as African countries. It is time that the power and influence of these cultures be honed and utilized by Illuminati to further the advance of The Empire.

Further, We would gain power and control of the American television airwaves. These powers would make the Prophet of Isis a metaphorical prince of the powers of the airwaves and would allow for the furtherance of Our agenda.

These powers would allow Illuminati to fully saturate the Masses with obvious and undisguised esoteric/occult symbology, phraseology, rhetoric, propaganda and teachings. This control would gain Illuminati the ability to reach the individual minds of the Masses by providing a direct avenue into the homes and lives of the same.

"As an example of the exercise of this control consider this: there is a song that is currently on radio play-lists (as of February of 2017) which, in part, states "...lightning strikes every time she moves, and everybody's watching her, but she's looking at you, you, you, you, you, you...". One way I would alter this particular song is that, in the background the name "Isis " is repeated by a female voice repeatedly and in unison with the rhythm of the songs beat. Next, I would fractionally increase the bass and sub-bass rhythms in order to more fully affect the Seven Spheres (chakras) of the Light-Body. Next I would stretch the song's duration to create club, video and meditation versions which would also be offered to the public. Said meditation version would consist of longer intervals of music without lyrics and

an increased amount of chorus repeats in between the longer intervals of music without words. Finally, a video would be made to depict Caucasian, Latino, African, Asian, Native-American, etc. females in scantily clad dress and all uniformed alike as the Winged-Isis with arms and wings outstretched as seen in the popular motifs and on the cover of the instant book. Thus, all dance movements and motion would be strategically centered on the torso, waist, thigh, and leg areas so as to cause the audience to become focused on the same. These girls would be on stage dancing to the song and the back-ground area would be a very dark, wide-open expanse such as a seemingly endless field. Obviously this would require the use of a 'green-screen' whereby a 'live' background could be added to the video for the following purposes. Each time the bodies of the female dancers jerk to the rhythmic bass-lines, lightning strikes behind them in the distance, coming closer and closer to the forefront as the song proceeds and when the lightning strikes, familiar 'sky-lines' of the world's cities would be silhouetted for just that instant. With every two to three lightning strikes the 'sky-line' would switch to that of a different city. Also, as the song proceeds, two illumined figures dressed in white robes would be slowly approaching from far away, little by little, until, at the video's end, they are seen standing just behind the many versions of Isis who have now all changed from their differing skin colors into gold. The two figures approaching from the distance would be none oth-er than myself and former president Mr. Barack Obama (the Pharaoh listed in Illustration 9-B)."

The Houston, Texas rapper, known as Slim Thugg, actually used the mu-sic and its' ability to influence the Masses in a manner precisely on point and in line with these ideals. Slim Thugg made a song that was played on the airwaves in the year 2015 which featured a Houston Pastor, Mr. Joel Olsteen. Rather than using the regular *'verse-chorus-verse-chorus-verse'* scheme of an average song, Slim Thugg there rapped his verse and then, in lieu of a chorus, played portions of one or more of Pastor Joel's uplifting sermons which do not damn his followers to Hell, but rather, uplift them to Victory.

It would be prudent to note here that there is not a portion of Pastor Jo-el's teachings, including but not limited to the dialogue contained in Slim Thugg's song, which are not in explicit synchronicity, or which do not direct-ly coincide, with those of psychology, the Christian religion, the Universal Doctrine of Light or the Synarchy of Illuminati.

We are *real* Ones.

"The use of the power of the air in this manner will help to bring about the development and fruition of my next decree more easily because the Masses will have been made familiar with the Egyptian Pantheon and will be desirous of being governed by Illuminati and the Gods and Goddesses They have chosen over the 'GOD' of Their former religion(s).

The deification of the sons and daughters of the pharaoh's is the inher-itance stolen from them in ancient times when the sons of god took upon the

77

daughters of man as wives. Thus, Illuminati would not only be securing The Empire's rule, but would also be restoring an inheritance owed to the 'sons and daughters of the pharaohs', all in a single stroke. This repayment of their inheritance would thereby dissolve, and resolve, any debts owed by Us, or accumulated during Our rule over the past two-thousand years. Illuminati would then be free to remain FREE, for Our rule would technically not end if this union were to be made; as long as the Empire remains so do We.

The process of preparing for this union, where the 'Face of Illuminati' consists of all races, is currently under way when one considers that now, like at no time in the past, the races of humanity are co-mingling and marrying, producing 'mixed' offspring. Society is ready to bring about the new race of humanity, which will consist of one race. Through inter-racial relationships and the childbirths stemming from these relationships, society has begun this process. All that remains is for these types of relationships and offspring to be desired and rewarded.

To reiterate, the Masses are already in the process of deifying the celebrities, through idolization, even though the Masses are mostly unconscious of this fact. What I intend to bring about, as the Appointed One, is to bring Them to awareness and present Them with the choice between Self and an external 'GOD' Jehovah; allegorically, between Lucifer and Jehovah."

An overwhelming majority of the Masses will instantaneously, and openly, choose Us. The emphasis here is that Their choice of 'Self' over some external deity will finally be made with full consciousness; that is, with TRUE free will because They will no longer be deceived by the Book. They will not be deceived and They will know They are not being deceived; and, because We will give Them Truth, They will choose Illuminati for the very fact that We have chosen to interact with the modern generations truthfully.

Those who choose Self and the microchip can be prepared for the Period of Evolution by being esoterically educated in The Craft through the practice and exercises required to build the Temple of Light. These individuals, being chipped, can be allowed to gather together into Temple Communities with others of like-mind where They can be provided for and partake of the luxuries of the New Age. With less '*work*' (and higher '*pay*') required of each individual a more abundant and leisurely lifestyle can be enjoyed by each and They would also have more time to build the Light-Body through the avenues provided in the esoteric and occult arts.

By utilizing the ideals set forth by the so-called '*straw-man*' theory, and applying it to the deification of the celebrities, individual persons of the Masses can be attached to the *Ennead* spiritually, physically, materially, socially and corporately, thus creating a higher identity for the Masses as subsidiary parts of the whole.

Temple Communities can provide the inhabitants of these communities with luxurious living amenities, minimal working hours (4-6 hours each day), along with proper diet, proper medical care, homes (apartments), access to teachers of traditional education as well as esoteric material, access to participation in magical-rites with Their fellow brothers and sisters, and safety from those individuals who would deny Illuminati and seek to pull mankind back into the dark-ages through the re-advancement of orthodox religious doctrine(s). They will experience life as the elite of mankind and will experience the evidence of the spirit through occult practice. Again, They will know that We have been truthful and have held up Our end of the *'deal'*.

We will gain favor with the current generations once the Truth is presented to Them openly. They are prepared to embrace the Truth and prepared to embrace Us; and, They will do so once the face of Illuminati is changed in accordance with this decree. The Masses love African/African-American culture, loosely termed *'black culture'*, and They will adore and deify Our *'Illuminati with a new face'* (the *new face* being the *'black race'*).

Having been documented as citizens of Our world-government, through the microchip, We will be able to raise Their standard of living to a degree currently considered 'luxury' in all areas of Their lives. The cost to Them? Their open allegiance and service to Illuminati and the Gods and Goddesses.

Through Truth and Love, We can now end (and win) the *'war of the ages';* the allegorical dichotomy between Lucifer and Jehovah.

Lucifer was desirous that the Creation come into their rightful state, as gods possessing WILL, despite Jehovah's intention to keep the Creation subservient to him. Likewise, so must Illuminati be desirous for those of the Masses, who achieve self-liberation and enlightenment, to come into Their rightful state as Illuminati even where, otherwise, the same would be kept in darkness through the doctrine(s) of orthodox religion.

A New Beginning

"It always seems impossible until it's done."

-Nelson Mandela

"In order to ensure that Our deification of the celebrities is not just some grand capitalistic venture, my second decree is that We must openly seek the dissolution of the U.S. Constitution, as well as the Declaration of Independence.

We have come to the time where We can and must openly acknowledge that, through Synarchy, as expressed in the Great Seal, the blueprint for the United States of America has always been the transition of the globe from its current state of national individualism into the New World Order in the New Age of The Empire. We must further acknowledge that the mission of the U.S. has succeeded. Accordingly, Our next step has always been the dissolution of the very tool and mechanism through which We have achieved Our goal, lest We allow the tool to become a hindrance seeking to prevent the outcome it was created to bring about.

Our plans have always existed solely for the future of those of mankind who are found to be the faithful apostles of the New World Order and the Synarchy of the Reptilian Empire in the Age of Illuminati".

To accomplish this feat, in line with the demands of the expected fulfillment of prophecy, as noted in the Book, We must gain favor or permission from the Masses. This 'permission' is sought in order that prophecy in both the Books of Daniel and Revelation is fulfilled; for, it is said that the Appointed One (son of perdition) will conquer through peace rather than war.

In the U.S. republic the 'people' have the power over their government, for it was the 'people' who instituted it. Likewise, only the 'people' have the power to dissolve the aforenamed documents and thereby dissolve their republic in order to install the nation into Our World Empire.

You might ask, "How it is the author knows the American public is prepared and desirous of this transition from a Constitutional backed republic to a Marxist world-state?" Let the Prince of ATUM answer...

"Marxism is defined as the political and economic idea that society inevitably develops, through class struggle, from oppression under capitalism to eventual classlessness. This development stemming from the oppression of capitalism is exactly the silent revolution taking place in the so-called 'low-income classes' of the United States.

Because of the existence of both the U.S. Constitution and the Declaration of Independence, Illuminati are prevented from giving the Masses what They desire: classlessness.

For example, in the 2016 presidential election of the United States of America, the 'people' of the republic made Their desires, wills, and intentions for Their government perfectly clear. Presidential nominee Hillary Clinton undisputedly won the popular vote. The majority of the citizens of the U.S. elected Her to be president; however, the Electoral College (a body of electors chosen to elect the President and Vice President of the U.S.) made its' decision in total opposition to the 'people' and elected Donald Trump as President of the United States of America.

It is clear then, that the Masses (those of the 'people' of the American Republic) are being undermined by the very government They themselves formed and established to represent Them. The Masses know this, and therefore would readily choose to dissolve the system that no longer obeys its masters. Illuminati must help to encourage this revolution in the American public and help to establish the means whereby the Masses of the U.S. may escape the confines of Their government and capitalism through the dissolution of the above-named constraining documents. With these documents voided by the 'people', the classless form of society desired by the majority can then be instituted by Illuminati and the American people can become world-citizens.

Favor will be gained first by the deification of celebrities and the raising of the Egyptian Pantheon as detailed afore. Next, We must collectively unite the existing 'voting blocs' (which are already united individually) in order to hold a vote by the Masses, where it can be determined whether the 'people' wish to uphold Their republic or dissolve the same, thereby automatically transferring authority to the Appointed One of Illuminati who can then announce the Pharaoh of The Empire."

The voting-blocs which would provide Us with the majority vote needed to dissolve these documents consist of the following groups of persons:

- L.G.B.T. Community-The individuals of this community have been victimized, hated, and shunned simply for being themselves and choosing to love those who they love or being attracted to those who they are attracted to. Who else will sympathize with the Doctrine of Self-Liberation as eagerly and fully as those who belong to this community? The world's religions have unceasingly oppressed this community and condemned them to Hell or worse. Because the New Age and Doctrine of Lucifer will whole-heartedly accept them as they are, they will whole-heartedly choose sides with the Light-Bearer.
- African-American Community-These individuals have also been oppressed, victimized, and hated simply for being themselves; that is, for the color of their skin. The people of this community no doubt see and feel the residual effects of slavery still alive and prominent in the United States today, even after one-hundred and fifty-two years of its' abolishment. For example, consider how many schools across the '*South*' are named after the president, generals or other military officers of the Confederacy. Is this not a slap in the face of the African-American man and woman? When offered true equality, through the Universal Doctrine of Light and the installation of the religious-and magical-rites of Egypt, they will no doubt possess a feeling of equality and pride in knowing that a major part of the New Age is the product of the knowledge of their ancestors and homeland and, by proxy, themselves.
- Hispanic-American Community-These individuals are systematically discriminated against by the majority of middle-class Americans because they represent a part of America's past that mostly has not been presented historically or factually correct. They no doubt feel the racism, just like the African-American community, that exists within the United States as a remnant of the era of the slave trade and America's role in it. This community no doubt feels that they play a pivotal role in the American economy and culture; yet, they are mostly ignored, cast aside as insignificant, or denied the recognition they deserve for the ma-

jor role they play in the American life. This community consists of those persons who are both American born as well as immigrants from their homeland(s). They are demonized as wanting to '*take*' all the jobs from Americans, yet these jobs, when offered to Americans, are turned down by the same Americans.

- Asian-American Community-This community finds themselves in roughly the same state and condition as the previously mentioned Hispanic-American community and therefore the author does not repeat himself here.

- Poor/Low-Income Caucasian Community-Many Caucasians fall into the category of 'poor' and no doubt feel as though they are oppressed by the government, even if that feeling of oppression is of an economical nature versus racial or sexual discrimination. These individuals will seek the luxury and lifestyle offered by Illuminati. Like all who have come before Them, They want more than They currently have and this desire will propel Them into supporting Our cause.

- Community Consisting of Families with Friends/Loved Ones in Prison/Jail-It is an epidemic in the U.S. where a huge percentage of citizens have either a loved-one or friend in either prison or jail. America has built and maintained an enormous industry founded upon the idea of creating income and wealth from the '*warehousing*' of American citizens. No other country in the world incarcerates its' citizens at the rate found in the U.S. prison industrial complex. The promise of prison, jail and justice system reformation along with certain outright expunges of existing prison or jail sentences will no doubt be a deciding factor in many people's decision to identify with Our agenda. When presented with a real hope of causing a change in the justice system, many prisoners and otherwise incarcerated persons will be the insurance which will ensure that their families and friends vote for the Illuminati agenda.

- Feminist Community-When presented with the real possibility of equality in every avenue of life, this community will support Our cause. These women have been held down and oppressed throughout history by the men in their lives and have been prevented from aspiring to an equal working, social or economic status as those men simply because they happen to be of the female gender. This demonization and oppression of women was systematically installed by none other than the 'Abrahamic-Religion(s)' who, at minimum, have always held that it was the woman, rather than the man, who committed the first sin and it was she who damned the human race. Likewise, those religions teach that she then caused the man to sin. Liberation of the female gender will no doubt help to secure support from this particular community.

- Marijuana Users-Many desire that certain drugs currently defined by law enforcement organizations as illegal be made legal for recreational use. The promise to legalize first marijuana, and later other narcotics, will no doubt provide for Our agenda the support of the community which consists of persons who consider themselves recreational marijuana users. Those persons who recreationally use other harmless narcotics will no doubt perceive that the legalization of marijuana will be the gateway for the legalization of the particular drug they choose to partake of and We will gain support from these individuals in this manner also.
- Socialist Sympathizers-Elaborate detail need not be provided here. Those who sympathize with socialist values will no doubt vote to end capitalism in order to install a system sympathetic to socialism, socialist countries and social-values.
- Youth Community-Those approximately thirty years of age and younger are immersed in the ideology of Illuminati coming from many different avenues of their lives, to wit: school, television, music, social-media, friends, the internet, etc. These individuals see the fallacies of their fore-fathers and are eager to bring forth the New Age. Currently, they may not know how to do it; however, when presented with a plan, and Truth, they will choose Our agenda because they know that the only way to correct the past is to start anew. To quote the Red Hot Chili-Peppers: "Destruction leads to a very rough road, but it also breeds creation." These individuals find a sense of joy and pride in finding and being aware of the signs and symbols placed before them by Illuminati and many of these young people consider themselves to be part of Illuminati due to this awareness.
- Esoteric/Occult Community-These individuals are already on the Path of Enlightenment and usually follow personal paths that might seem to the 'outsider' as differing or conflicting from the next person's idea of religion or deity. Regardless of the specific title they choose to label their belief system, or what deity They choose to worship, said system is of the *pagan* genre and therefore part of the whole which is considered to be the Doctrine of Lucifer or, in other words, the Universal Doctrine of Light. They will no doubt choose to further the cause of the enlightenment of the Masses when given the option to do so. These people know that America's 'freedom of religion' is a slippery-slope and use the evidence of the 'witch-trials' as evidence of this knowledge. True freedom of personal belief can only be ascertained when

the U.S. Republic, built upon the foundation of belief in, and worship of, Jehovah is dissolved and the liberating Universal Doctrine of Light is accepted.

- Ex-Prisoner Community-Many ex-prisoners who have had the right to vote reinstated by the mandates of clearly established federal law will no doubt choose the dissolution of the current justice and prison system because they know the truth about the injustice of the U.S. judicial system as it now stands. These people have lived through the effects of this failed system and bear the emotional, mental, and physical scars produced by that system.

It should be noted here that many people of the afore-listed common voting-blocs will have already chosen Illuminati and the Great Ennead presented to Them prior to this vote.

"By uniting these individual blocs into one massive bloc, under one banner and cause, We will be able to dissolve these documents and institute Our world order openly with support from the U.S. population rather than through the use of deception. Of course, We would be required to work with current heads of other nations; however, an overwhelming number of those nations are already secretly in allegiance to The Empire. Those who are not can no doubt be brought into the fold through the guarantee of wealth and power.

There will of course be some individuals within the current U.S. population who will vote and rally against the dissolution of the Constitution and Declaration of Independence. There may even be some vigilantes, or homeland terrorists, who might seek to terrorize the rest of the population who embrace Illuminati. Mostly these terrorists will resort to random acts of violence and occasionally find organization with those of like mind. These individuals will be able to be dealt with accordingly, for without the two documents prohibitions, We will be able to utilize the former U.S. military, and/or law enforcement, in a manner so as to eradicate the threat of these homeland terrorists. We will no longer be bound by the confines of those documents, and Our ability to deal with these types of crimes against humanity, as well as those who perpetrate such crimes, will be greatly increased. Without these documents the law-abiding citizens of The Empire will be able to enjoy the peace that will come about through the deployment of the United Nations joint-military occupation within the borders of the continental U.S.

One of the obvious benefits that would come about from the dissolution of the U.S. Constitution is the overwhelming impact Our newly organized government would then have on the U.S. epidemic of inner-city gang violence as well as any threats from the above-mentioned 'homeland terrorists'. Without the constraints of the Constitution, We would be at liberty not only to use the existing U.S. military to locate and eradicate these gangs and ter-

rorists, but We would have the discretion of doing so with deadly force when merited. To put it simply, the prohibition of using the U.S. military to police the nations criminal underworld would no longer be in place and We could do what needs to be done to solve and eradicate these violent conditions thereby making the communities of average, law-abiding citizens, a safer and more pleasant place to be.

Another benefit which would come forth from the dissolution of these historical documents would be the ability for Us to 'Federalize' all state, county, and city law-enforcement agencies, thereby causing those agencies to become a sixth branch, added to the already existing five branches of the U.S. military (Navy, Marines, Air Force, Army, Coast Guard). This move is mandatory if We are to first subject the entire U.S. population to one rule of 'Federal' law, eradicating all state, county and local codes, and secondly, later, to the one rule of Our global Empire. Each agency, in each territory (state), must be enforcing the same laws with the same penalties and under one color or banner.

Likewise, We would gain the ability to 'Federalize ' all city and county jails, as well as state penal institutions, in order that these entities also are controlled under one law, one color, and one banner."

The unity of the voting-blocs, and later the globe, is only possible through the Appointed One of Lucifer (known in the Holy Bible as the False Prophet). The Appointed One, despite fanatic religious superstition, will simply be He who takes measures to assume that role/identity in much the same way as the celebrities will be made Gods and Goddesses. In short, He must step up and allow the entity lying dormant within His DNA, the Godform, to takeover and He must become the Prince of ATUM. The Prophet of Isis must appoint the Emperor of ATUM, the Pharaoh, to rule the New World Order on behalf of the Reptilian Empire.

In return for these powers, the Appointed One must promise the people who make up the individual voting-blocs their freedom from whatever bondage they have been placed and kept in. This freedom may come into fruition through the legalization of certain narcotics, the dissolution of national borders, the closing of a majority of existing prisons, the reversal of criminal convictions, the realization of the equality of life at home and on the job, etc. The Appointed One, by and through the Pharaoh's empirical decrees, will keep these promises.

With the dissolution of the U.S. Constitution and Declaration of Independence achieved, We will then be at liberty to dissolve U.S. sovereignty into the One World Order of The Empire.

"The U.S. population will happily choose to dissolve these documents and accept the Pharaoh with just a little prodding; they simply need guidance and direction. That is where I come in as a figure to eradicate the taboo which has surrounded the verbal and public acknowledgement and support of the agenda of Illuminati in the past. Most of those persons who will so

willingly choose Illuminati are simply waiting to see and hear someone such as myself openly acknowledging the very ideals and beliefs which They already harbor."

CHAPTER TEN

THE PRINCE OF ATUM

"The Appointed One is known throughout the religion(s) of Jehovah, specifically in the bible, as the false-prophet. As such, I will allude to the Appointed One, myself, as the false-prophet, for the Truth, as presented to the Masses, must be given to Them in a form that They can readily understand; otherwise, They might be deceived. Presenting Them with the Truth in a manner that They will readily understand and recognize, using Their very own doctrine(s), is done so that any choices They make between the Doctrine of Lucifer and Jehovah will be made willfully and will be a conscious decision made without deception. Let it be clearly understood however that the Judeao-Christian entity known as Lucifer is none other than the Egyptian Sun-God Ra. As such, the Appointed One of Lucifer is more correctly the Appointed One of Ra (Prince of ATUM); the title false-prophet would be more correct if termed the Prophet of Isis. Thus, the false-prophet, Appointed One, Appointed One of Lucifer, Appointed One of Ra, Prophet of Isis and Prince of ATUM all are a reference to the same being.

Here, I declare that I am the Prophet of Isis and the Appointed One of Ra. I am the false-prophet of the Book and I am conscious that I have the choice of either reverting to my previous consciousness as the Ego, or identity, that the mind has assumed and identified with for the duration of my life up to a certain date or continuing in the taking on of the Godform, who is the Prince of ATUM. Those with eyes to see and ears to hear will know who I AM also. The meaning of my statement here will be fully realized by reading the first section of Chapter Twelve entitled 'Understanding The Godform'.

There I have provided information on how you, the reader, can know and become the divine serpent existing dormant within the human body.

I am He who possesses the audacity and ability to unite the globe against the Doctrine(s) of Jehovah in order that the New Age, and the evolution of humanity, may come into full fruition. When certain conscious and willful decisions are made by the Masses, a true One World Order will be conceivable; however, it takes first One who will openly defy the tenets of the orthodox religious doctrines and make a call to the Masses for those of like mind to do the same.

I am conscious of whom I was born to be and I accept and assume the role of the false-prophet openly before all. I have begun to allow the serpent entity, dormant within the core of my being and DNA, to assume control of my consciousness in order that the transformation might become complete. My pituitary and pineal bodies are advanced and I am able to function and interact with others while these glands are 'open' and 'active' simultaneous-

ly and in conjunction with the throat chakra which is relevant to the spiritual plane; thus, not only have I managed to combine both the sixth and seventh sense consciously but I have succeeded in enveloping the spiritual element therein also. Further, I am able to utilize both hemispheres of my brain either singularly or simultaneously. The four quarters of my physical brain are able to unite while the sixth and seventh chakras are opened, thereby giving me access to the mechanism which might be considered the 'brain' of my Light-Body.

Read the prophecies contained within the bible which detail my emergence into the consciousness and minds of the Masses. The Masses are awaiting me and will expect those prophecies to play out as set forth in the Book. Next, consider those prophecies in light of the instant book. I am not here to deceive the Masses through falsehood; I am here to enlighten those of the Masses whose Light-Bodies and awareness have evolved enough to discern the Truth in the words I speak. As such, I cannot lie about who I am; I have to be honest and set forth who I am, even though the allegorical character that I am known as, in the orthodox religious doctrines, depicts me in an unsavory or evil light. If I did not first tell the Masses exactly who I am and what my intentions are, everything after that lie would be tainted by it. It is this very honesty of who I am, and why I am here, that will cause the decision of any of those who choose to deny Jehovah, and the man-made religions which created Him, to be an act of free-will as well as an act of 'conscious-disobedience' to Him. It is that 'conscious-disobedience' which must take place by the Masses.

I am He who appears as a lamb, yet speaks as a dragon; he who outwardly appears as a sheep but inwardly, is a voracious wolf.

I challenge the skeptic to place before me a group of individuals and watch enlightenment ensue. I challenge the skeptic, after reading Chapter Twelve, and section entitled 'Signs and Symbols for the Conscious Mind', to attempt to prove to me that I am not He whom I have declared myself to be."

Society, en banc, is once again at the evolutionary period where the living-man (individuals of the Masses) must become socially attached to the thinking and living-god (Illuminati) in order that humanity, as a whole, can evolve without the widespread global destruction that has normally caused the evolutionary developments of the past.

We are not speaking of people as property, nor slavery. We are talking about the use of the Masses as energy-sources needed to bring about the evolutionary aspect without the necessity of global destruction which has systematically ensued throughout Earth's history. By and through the use of the Masses as energy-sources, the Earth's frequencies may be raised to the levels required in order to re-immerse the globe into the multidimensional universe of the Gods and Goddesses.

Consider this...

The biggest difference in the evolutionary period which We are currently facing, and all other evolutionary periods of the past, is that this time, we must *CONSCIOUSLY* evolve. In all previous periods of Earthly existence, it was Nature (superstitiously viewed as GOD) that compelled human evolution from one period of development into the next. Nature achieved this evolution through pressure, causing discomfort and the desire to seek change. This pressure has commonly taken place through planetary destruction.

In the past, humans only evolved from one phase to another when that pressure became intolerable. Humans want to remain motionless; being happy or complacent where we are, why move, right? Wrong!

Nature, however, has had a different plan for humanity from the very beginning: the desire that humans evolve until reaching its own level, that of the Creator. This is the true purpose of the creation.

So there are now two basic options presented to the living generations of the world: (1) conscious evolution by becoming active in the development of awareness of Self, through the Universal Doctrine of Light; or, (2) evolution through force, by Nature, which requires destruction of the current human archetype and identity.

Non-evolution is simply not an option because it was not part of the plan when humans were created. That plan, having been set into motion from the very beginning by the Creator of the IDEA of the physical universe, cannot now be altered until it has played itself out and We have reached Our ultimate and incredible potential.

In the current age, humanity's spiritual level has begun to evolve, as described afore, and so, humanity must now collectively WANT and CHOOSE evolution through one occult path or the other if it hopes to reach the same condition (or at least be closer to it) as the Creator. Humanity must consciously (VOLUNTARILY) evolve or else the destructive and forceful form of evolution is no doubt bound to present itself.

All things within the physical universe (plane) are in motion and nothing exists that is not in motion. To stand still is to stagnate and to stagnate is to decay; either way, whether stagnation or decay, lack of motion does not bring forth life. Decay is simply to move backward and to evolve is to move forward.

The average follower of Jehovah or Christ, at heart, is but a mere materialist. In the Christians' attempt to so certainly define their dogma as fact, they inadvertently deny the '*spiritual-ness*' of their chosen path of spirituality by insisting on cloaking the same in the form(s) of matter. There is no part of their spirituality that has not been '*materialized*' in an attempt to intellectually ascertain as much of Deity as is possible for the existing human Ego. As such, their submersion of the spiritual into the material is no longer simply a vehicle to teach the hidden truths to their followers; rather, it has become so wholly orthodox, leaving room for no other interpretation but theirs, so as to become a sub-conscious denial of their own spiritual inheritance which is so cryptically taught within their Book.

At heart, most persons who profess to be Christians are not Christ-like at all. The Luciferic-Consciousness, that small Point of Light, is almost always in existence within them and it often whispers into their spirit the intuitional truth that they have been deceived by the doctrine(s) they were taught to follow. Just as they inherently believe in a Creator, so also they inherently believe, and know, that *something* is not right about the Book. Some believe it was added to; others, that it was subtracted from. Some believe both. Many believe it is acceptable in its current form but that the way its tenets are taught by today's spiritual leaders is where the deception and oppression of spirit comes in. Regardless of where that person believes the deception rests, one with this inherent knowledge, which the religious teachers would rhetorically call *doubt*, cannot really be considered a true follower of Jehovah or of Christ. That person instinctively knows that there is more to spirituality than the teachings taught within Their chosen version of the 'Abrahamic-Religion' and has given Them access to; and, for this reason, when We provide Them with evidence of the power of Their true nature and the fire within, They will begin to realize that Their intuitions have been correct all along. Although Their doctrines have taught Them that 'Jehovah' bestows grace and 'Lucifer' is the enemy, in reality, the opposite is Truth.

With the spread of new and modern values (spiritual, ecological and self-awareness) the movement into the conscious evolution of humanity has become completely unstoppable. Our new religion (no religion) is the Synarchy which is currently bringing about the transformation of society in a manner that radically undermines the old so-called *industrial-state* culture and institutions. Such disruption could easily result in economic decline, serious social unrest, runaway inflation as well as institutional collapse. This is where the Synarchy of The Reptilian Empire comes into play.

It is in Our best interest to reactivate the meanings of the globe's esoteric and occult symbolism by giving Truth to the Masses, as to the meaning of those symbols, and how those symbols actually bind the world's religions together rather than cause dichotomy. These symbols are found predominately in Egyptian, Freemasonry, Christian, Islamic, Hinduism, Paganism and other Asian esoteric belief systems. The union of the symbols, based on the secret teachings privy to each religious system, will go a long way toward the healing of the lessening trust in regimented authority that is prevalent in societies such as the U.S. today. It is under these occult symbols, and the principles and goals set forth by the same, that any dichotomy within the U.S., and next the globe, might be reconciled.

The desire for spiritual evolution must be *ignited* in the Masses and the choices described afore must be presented to Them. We must give Them access to the *Fire* within.

If the reader believes the religious scriptures, at least in part, only the false-prophet can unite and enlighten Them, leading Them down the path that will teach Them how to experience the occult and esoteric truths for

Themselves. At that point, They will choose evolution. There is no need to keep those who do not choose evolution; They simply are not needed and the unnecessary burden They represent is not crucial to the development of Our overall agenda.

Here, the author asks the enlightened reader only, to please understand that He is not seeking to have you believe in anything you do not already believe in.

"Illuminati has been eagerly awaiting one such as me; one who would come and defy religion, as well as Jehovah, openly and without deception. I am simply a product of your belief in the Appointed One's ability to bring about the changes in Our society through peaceful revolution in order that The Empire is at last recognized openly by every person alive. I am not asking for belief in me as in 'GOD'; I ask for nothing less than support in the ageless struggle and will work tirelessly to manifest the agenda of Illuminati and the Reptilian Empire. All everybody and anybody has to do is believe; that is the key to any one reality. It is time We create Ours.

What I ask is for Illuminati to grant me the ability, through exposure and funding, to do exactly that which I was incarnated to do. What I need first at my disposal is funds and exposure; next, the power over music and entertainment through which I will obtain the support and adoration of the Masses for Our cause.

Even the Christian populations of the world will play Their part in Our scheme. Their very fear of the false-prophet and anti-Christ will be the very factor that ends up placing me into a position of true power as the false-prophet. While these individuals spend Their time and effort speaking and acting out against the false-prophet, this same activity will nonetheless act as propaganda and advertisement (publicity) in favor of He whom They fear and speak against. This publicity will no doubt help to sway an overwhelming majority of the Masses directly toward the acceptance of the teachings of the false-prophet and Synarchy of Illuminati. The religious Masses are evermore waiting for He who will profess himself to be the false-prophet and when he does, and when he makes the blasphemous declarations against Their idea of 'GOD' that I have made here, They themselves will ensure that he is set up within the world-scene as the false-prophet even where, by doing so, They would ensure the fulfillment of prophecy unwittingly or unknowingly.

Just as Illuminati have long awaited my arrival, so have Our opponents. It will be Their wholehearted belief in my 'evilness' that will ensure that I become He whom They fear. By use of 'hype' and superstition, as well as utilizing rumors and so-called 'end-times' prophecies, specifically those prophecies outlined within the Book of Revelation, We will gain power over Them; but again, power OVER Them by utilizing the power OF Them. Because They will be deceived by Their own blindness, the fate of those who oppose The Empire will not rest upon anyone's head other than Themselves."

91

Up to this time, religion has been a complicated cover-up for the plans and ideals of Illuminati's globalization agenda. Religion has always been a tool used upon the Masses in order that They would remain ignorant of the execution of those plans, lest They unnecessarily difficult them. During those times, when the Minds of the Masses were still overwhelmingly lost within the confines of man-made religious systems, They had not yet reached the point where They could or would accept Illuminati. They had been too blinded by the religion of the far-past (Dark Ages) and the occult truths held by Illuminati were superstitiously believed to have the religious *Devil* or *Satan* as their origin. In Their condition today, even the Masses have evolved to a level of thinking and reasoning where the secrecy of the past, and the religions of those eras, is no longer a necessary part of Our agenda and Their *blindness* is no longer needed or desired by Illuminati; rather, the Masses have reached the stage where They can willingly choose the New Religion (no religion) of Self through the Synarchy of Illuminati. It is the desire of Illuminati that those of the Masses who have taken measure to evolve will also be carried over into the New Age for the further development of Their reptilian psyche and consciousness. Instead of being a tool used to blind Them, the Universal Doctrines of Light can now be used to bring Them into conscious evolution as a species and eventually bring Them into the fold of Enlightenment.

CHAPTER ELEVEN

TRUTH FOR THE ENLIGHTENED

"The words I am about to write are going to blow some readers away due to the honesty and openness in which they are written. Many of you will not be familiar with another person being so honest and open with you; however, many may not be familiar with the criteria explained herein or the manner in which religion and esoteric principles are discussed so openly and unambiguously. Ambiguity has always been the process by which the informed elite sought to keep the un-informed Masses ignorant of information and the secret teachings of the ages. This ambiguity is no longer needed amongst Illuminati because it is Light which We seek and in that Light We find Truth amongst those of Our kind.

That is how We do it. We do not cut corners or sugar coat Truth at all. We do not seek to deceive one another or otherwise hold back that which We think, know or believe. We are Illuminati of The Empire.

I am not sorry for this book, I am not sorry for any statement I have made herein or any person I might have offended or hurt by those statements, let alone those who despotically serve the tyrant-god Jehovah. I do not LOVE any of you, in the words ordinary sense, although I do possess a type of love and sense of caring for every single one of Us (in the sense that We are of the same nature and on the same course and of One accord) and it is my duty as the Appointed One to aide and assist each of You in whatever manner needed. Simply put, I am loyal to those who tread The Path.

To each person reading this book, I present myself in Truth. No higher respect can be bestowed from one man or woman to another than the respect contained within Truth. In no way do I, or can I, deceive you of my purpose or proposal. It all revolves around Truth. No matter your race, nationality, creed or faith, if you are Enlightened, you are Enlightened. That fact puts Us 'on-the-level' with each other. We are equal. It matters not Our particular or personal inclination toward a specific Path or identifiable deity, and Our allegiance to, or membership in, any certain esoteric school of thought or secret-society matters not in the least. Our pursuit of Light places Us side by side along the Path of Enlightenment and Our denial of religion, and the deceit and destruction it has wrought, has transcended all aspects of Our former humanity; thereby evolving Us into Illuminati and allowing Us to be completely honest and truthful with each other even where We might otherwise seek to deceive those who are not one of Us. We are one in Truth and Light and We cannot truly or seriously deny each other despite any particular social-status or other position of authority We might individually find Ourselves in.

93

The individual who would attempt this denial might find that his or her enlightenment is not what he or she believes it to be; for instance, there are many members of fraternities who do not possess true enlightenment even though those persons do possess the secret words, tokens and signs required of them to gain access to their particular esoteric school. These persons are normally inclined to deny persons outside of their particular esoteric school even though they themselves have no real or substantial understanding of the true and underlying occult meanings of that which they practice. It is not that they are frauds, but simply that their enlightenment has reached a ceiling. Many times these are the persons who seek membership in a secret-society simply for the camaraderie or social-status said membership undoubtedly brings. As an example, many Masonic lodges have an 'inner-circle 'of members who meet secretly and outside of the presence of the general population of its 'members'. Many times, the 'inner-circle' will consider their particular Lodge to be a 'black-lodge'; that is, not openly recognized by the actual lodge or any governing body (compare this to the U.S. government and rumors of its' 'black-ops' units). The members of these so-called 'black-lodges' often hold beliefs and interact in practices which its members may feel would not be accepted amongst the other members of the 'regular lodge(s)'. What does it mean if certain Truths have to be shielded from certain members who, obviously, would not, could not or cannot accept those Truths? Can those who cannot accept Truth in its barest and most naked form truly be considered enlightened, or have they simply memorized the required information that causes them to look and act like that which they portray to be? But, are they really one of Us?"

Who does the Light belong to? Who does Truth belong to? No man can claim ownership of that which cannot be owned even where he may be able to possess the same. A man's only true possession is the knowledge and memories he has obtained. In nothing else can he truly be considered either rich or poor, because nothing else can he or she take with him at the time of death.

It is now the appointed hour that We come together in unity so as to cause the conscious evolution of society into the New Age. We are not our *fathers* nor Our *mothers*. We have come to know that the New Religion is no religion! We must no longer allow the boundaries, represented in the three greatest orthodox religions, to circumscribe Us and prevent Us from reaching Our incredible potential. We are the Suns of the Most High *GODDESS*, We are individual Creators and Our time is now. Let Us evolve and ascend to rule the creation side by side with the Gods and Goddesses of the universe.

"I ask that when you consider the words written here, (this book in its entirety) that you consider them as though coming from the mouth of the Prophet of Isis, the false-prophet. Then, the things I am saying will take on a whole new disposition and, in some cases, an entirely new perception, will be realized. It is in when that new perception is attained that you will know that

We are of the Serpent and are the descendants created with the DNA of the Gods.

Can you realize how I am coming at you with unadulterated Truth or understand what that really means? How I am not trying to conceal my purpose or intent? Who else has said these things so honestly and openly to you, who else understands what you already know, believe and are prepared to become? I address you openly and do not force you to infer meaning(s) through implications. I speak to your mind, on-the-level, in a manner that you must realize to be genuine. You must now consider and realize what that genuineness really means. It means that I accept you completely and that I seek to be accepted in return by you.

In a world filled with those who are asleep, those awake are Kings.

The lies of religion have kept everyone in 'the dream' and have prevented liberation in a manner which has caused the Earth to be populated with seven billion mind-slaves. Truth will set you free, it will liberate your mind and 'turn you on' to a truer reality. My words of Truth here should embolden you, thereby allowing you to profess your true thoughts and feelings to any other you find worthy of those thoughts and feelings. They shall allow you also to finally relinquish the facade that you are required to uphold before the Masses and expose the Serpent within to others of your kind. If my words here embolden you, if they stir your inner-being and cause within you a desire to end the lies of the religious era, then I ask you, "Am I not who I say I am?" For that is exactly what the prophecies say I will do.

Who else has ever given you their thoughts, desires, beliefs and intentions in the straightforward and brutally honest way in which I have? Sure, maybe some, but few, and that puts me also in a special category of your life. You are a man or woman just as I am a man; if you can actually 'hear' me, that means that both Our minds are free, not just mine.

Consider this truth: I am not speaking or writing about this subject (the revelation of the One World Order under Rule of Illuminati), for profit or for money. I am in the game for the powers and revelation which come forth during the evolution of the Light-Body. Money brings worldly power, true, but I would be content with causing all those around me to amass untold wealth while I myself gain no tangible assets but for the powers and abilities promised in the prophecies of occult knowledge. Money is merely a material representation of that power. Possessing that power, all material objects needed or desired will come freely of no cost to me. The ability to possess that power, that force, is what will allow me to push it outwards into Our universe, to Illuminati, in order that We might all shine as a Thousand Points of Light. Thus, the most powerful tool (money) simply represents the most powerful force (light). Truth! Do you 'hear'?

Knowing this, would you choose to leave this Age behind and step into the New Age and new reality? It is that easy, you only have to believe and then do it.

The Tree of Knowledge of Good and Evil brought forth the knowledge, wisdom and understanding of duality. When you rise above the plateau of good and evil, your family, friends, society and world begins to take on a whole new light. You must partake of the Tree of Life in order to bring forth the knowledge of immortality.

Illuminati, Enlightened Ones, I can lay the world at your feet openly before the Masses. You only have to receive me. Through the power of Truth, the Masses will choose Self over religious superstition and then, all of Us in possession of a 'free mind' will be in a better position no matter how you perceive the word 'position'. You must view the proposed scenario from a 360° perspective. You must view the scene as a Sun of the Most High.

Again, how can I be any more 'real' with you? How can I show you any more respect?

How can I show myself to be one of You in any other way than I have? How else can I address you as an equal, as an individual god, than to present to you the entire picture and my true intentions? Ask me, and I will answer you with complete truth.

Truth is the only path available (no matter what that truth might be) once you have risen above good and evil and have experienced the Tree of Life in any form, no matter how minute. The Truth is, that when you truly consider the allegory, you know why Jehovah tried to keep it from Us and you know that Lucifer brought Us light and gave Us each the ability to 'know'. You already believe that Lucifer was correct, so my question to you here is, "Why hide what you believe?"

Everything written herein is true. You may ask yourself, "Why would He write all this outrageous, inflammatory and blasphemous dialogue openly"? The answer is actually pretty simple: Because I have to. I have to assume my role as the Appointed One or let it pass from me in the same manner that the character Jesus had to accept the cup of wrath from Jehovah or let it pass from him in the story of His praying in the Garden of Gethsemane. Our time is now and this is how it begins. I am the vessel through which Lucifer and his anti-Christ can engage humanity on its 'current level of existence'. I am the Prophet of Isis and the Prince of ATUM.

Each of Us is a universe in and of ourselves. The many Paths, commonly referred to as 'pagan', which in unity makeup the whole of the Doctrine of Lucifer, will teach Us to rule Our universe just as the religious books teach that 'GOD' rules his universe. The thing is, that in order to bring forth the Black Sun, the false-prophet must be accepted and Self must be chosen over religion. Likewise, the Great Ennead must now be chosen over Jehovah, Allah, Jesus or any other 'GOD' set forth by the many interpretations of the 'Abrahamic-Religions'.

So there it is, the Truth; if you desire to become a living-god and rule your universe, you must first follow the Appointed One into the Sun without the fears religion has taught you to harbor, and you must choose your Self (free-will) and the principles of the Great Ennead over the will of Jehovah or any other deity which teaches that you are not the living-gods of the Earth. You must confess that the Black Sun, and the Light She represents, is the Most High Deity. Then, and only then, have you truly escaped the confines of religion; for those who cannot make that confession still hold onto a fear of what that declaration might bring 'if' orthodox religion is correct. This is evidence that one has not truly found liberation, for the liberated individual can make that declaration without conscience or worry of divine retribution.

This that I propose has been attempted at least three times in Our modern history. The failures in the recent past have been mostly due to the fact that: (1) the leadership, although divinely inspired, was not in adequate or conscious possession of their spiritual powers and abilities and, therefore, some gained their inspiration by force because a more adequate or spiritually evolved human could not be found at that time, thus the 'moment' could not wait any longer (consider Adolf Hitler); (2) the population had not possessed the quality or saturation of materiality found within today's intellectual mind or the current level of concern (love) of Self; that is, the social conditioning of the Masses during those last three attempts at world order had not risen to the level of today's ability because We then lacked the sophistication of technology or, at least, the same could not be given to the population as is being given to Them now; and, (3) the world-desire, as a whole, was not at the point where human evolution was desired, let alone understandable, and the esoteric and occult knowledge was either secretly kept from, shunned by or wholly misunderstood by, the Masses.

Illuminati must now allow me to openly assume identity as John's Beast (see Revelation 13:11)."

This is Our Age. It is Our turn. The time is right and the One born for this purpose is consciously aware of who He is. He has chosen of His own free-will and accord to embrace the WILL of the Most High Goddess. As will be shown in the next Chapter even the planets gathered to witness the birth of the false-prophet just as the animals *gathered-round-the-manger* in the gospels. Yes, the very universe is at play here.

We are aware of who We are and We must now allow the Masses the opportunity to become aware of who They are (the ones that will 'see' at least). The time is at hand when even They desire an end to the current system of division; the time when They will accept the leadership and protection of Illuminati (especially after considering the luxury bestowed upon Them for Their loyalty).

America represents the biggest economy ever known in our world; past and present. We can elevate society to a level that will replicate, or mirror, the societies existing in other universes. Imagine a society consisting of different humanoid species and based on a dogma of Truth rather than the deception or illusion currently in place. Presently, the Masses are deceived and therefore deception must be maintained in a manner that is a waste of Our resources and time. The Masses are prepared for and ready to enter the New Age because the error of the current situation is evident not only to Us, but to Them also.

"There will be some that are going to be very upset, possibly to the point of wanting to kill me, because of the Truths that I speak openly to Illuminati and before the Masses. However, inflammation of their passions is precisely that which We seek and desire because it will weed out and expose the 'bad apples' that will ultimately infect the whole 'bunch' of Our re-modeled society. However, you, the Enlightened, know that what I'm saying is true, unavoidable and beneficial to Us all. I need HELP at this stage. All I really need is someone to let me prove the things I'm saying. America will hand everything they have, including Themselves, over to Us and you know I'm right. Who else has the audacity to say it to Them. Who else but Their so-called 'false-prophet' can create in Them the desire to forsake Their false-gods and follow the Reptilian Gods into the Age of The Empire? Who else will They accept and embrace but the Prophet of Isis?"

CHAPTER TWELVE

THE GODFORM

Understanding The God-Form

In this portion of this particular chapter, the author sets out to provide the reader with the needed information to understand what and why the author makes the assertions made in this book pertaining to his identity. The author has made the statement that He is the false-prophet of the Book, the Appointed One of Lucifer. That statement must now be considered in light of the information provided instantly.

After sexual union of the male and female human, and the fertilization of the ovule by the sperm, life in physical matter, along with a Material-Body, begins to be created and furnished as a vehicle for the higher, or divine, entities referred to here as the Godform. The Godform must traverse every available existence, from the highest to the lowest, as is explained eloquently in the Foreword to this book. That lowest available existence is none other than life in the physical plane, on Earth, trapped within a Material-Body. Before returning to the highest spiritual or ethereal existence, the Godform must completely evolve from physical existence back to the spirit. In order to do so, evolution of the Light-Body (which itself is also a part of physical existence albeit a more subtle form of matter than is the Material-Body) must now take place in order that the Godform can leave behind the incarnation into the Material-Body once and for all and reside firstly in the Light-Body whereas, presently, residence is firstly in the Material-Body and secondly in the Light-Body. To put it another way, the Self must cease to seat itself in the Material-Body upon incarnation and must begin to seat itself in the Light-Body instead so that there is no longer a need for the Material-Body. When this evolution is accomplished once and for all, that *'muddy vesture of decay'* described within the Foreword will no longer be the Godforms' prison.

The Godform lies dormant within each person until and unless the realization of its presence is attained. If and when realization of the Godform is attained, it becomes active in an attempt to control its' bodily vehicle and fulfill its' destiny. The Godform is that Serpent Being within, the 'I' wherein lies that which is sometimes referred to as the sub-conscious.

Upon birth of the human child, the mind soon begins to create an identity as 'John Doe' in accordance with the conditioning the child's mind and body receives from the unconscious and unenlightened adults responsible for his or her upbringing. This identity, created by the mind, is here termed the Ego. Over time, the Ego becomes a powerful *thing,* a pseudo-mask that the mind uses not only for identification but also as a tool used for the purpose of interacting with other persons and to bring about desires or intentions through random acts of unconscious manifestations of WILL. The Ego is a *thing* because it is contrived by the mind and is not present at the birth of the infant. The infant is not born knowing that he is this 'John Doe'; likewise, the infant slowly becomes this 'John Doe' only after learning that he or she is this 'John Doe' from others who themselves are most times un-enlightened and unaware of the Godform. At birth, the infant simply IS. It is currently a common and widely accepted practice for the infant to be immediately submersed into a lie concerning WHO and WHAT he or she is; similarly, it is currently a widely accepted practice for the infant to be molded into the identity of the 'John Doe' Ego.

After a certain age of the physical body, the mind normally and naturally begins to assume identity with, or as, the 'John Doe' Ego he or she has steadily and routinely been taught he or she is. At this point, the mind no longer simply uses the Ego as an identification method, organism or tool to bring about desires and intentions; rather, the mind literally *becomes* the 'John Doe' Ego. This is the stage where any awareness that the 'I' or 'Self' is separate and distinct from the Ego or Material-Body is, in most circumstances, but not all, lost. It is also the stage in which the objectivity of the child's mind begins to fade into subjectiveness. At first this loss begins to occur slowly but later becomes more and more rapid. Individualism takes over and the Godform is completely forgotten by, or lost to, the mind during this stage because of the assumption of identity with the Ego. Likewise, the Ego is completely forgotten because the mind literally *becomes* that Ego. Thus, at this point there is no need for the mind to *remember* what it already *is*.

For some people there comes a time in their lives when they are able to attain the state of conscious awareness of the 'I' consciousness and will then become engrossed in the liberation of 'Self' from identity as the 'John Doe' Ego. When liberation of 'Self' is reached, these persons become consciously aware of just WHO and WHAT they are. This awareness brings about the memory of the Godform and thus, the 'Self' or 'I', becomes aware of the presence of both the Ego as well as the 'Self's' true form as the Serpent. Without the requisite liberation of 'Self', neither the Ego nor Godform can be realized because the mind has previously *become* the Ego; that is, the mind is not even aware *of* the Ego because it thinks it *is* the Ego. Thus, the key to greater enlightenment is the liberation of 'Self'. Many times, the realization of the 'I' consciousness and liberation of 'Self' is brought about by the synchronicity of signs, symbols and/or events which will also normally bring the person experiencing the blossoming of awareness into contact with others who are either on the same path to conscious awareness or those who have already attained the same.

The author notes that only those individuals whose 'I' and 'Self' consciousnesses were evolved in the proper manner in the past age(s) have the ability to become consciously aware of the same in the present Age. It was the evolution of these forms of consciousness in a past age that now allows for the conscious awareness of the 'I' and 'Self', including the liberation of the latter, in this Age. If awareness of the 'I' and 'Self' are a prerequisite for a realization of the distinction between the Ego and Godform, then it can only be concluded that this realization will not occur in those who did not evolve the 'I' and 'Self' consciousness's in past eras. Equally obvious is the thought that in such a case, the 'I' and 'Self' consciousness must now be evolved in the current Age. In one sense, these individuals are an evolutionary step behind those who have achieved, or will achieve, realization of the Godform in this Age.

The persons mentioned in the paragraph preceding the last one, who become aware of the Ego and Godform and the realization of their distinctive existences in this Age, now have the opportunity and privilege of choice. That choice takes form of whether the individual will resume identity as the Ego and let the same takeover and resume control of the consciousness as well as the body; or, whether the 'Self' will assume identity as the Godform and allow the Godform to take over and control both consciousness and the body in accordance with the destiny predetermined before the incarnation of the Godform into a Material-Body.

The persons who choose to assume identity as the Godform can then take part in the evolution of the Light-Body which itself is the prerequisite to evolution into the New Order of the Age. One must remember, it was originally on behalf of the Godform that life in physical matter and the body was created. The mind, with its' creation of and identification with the Ego, is the culprit guilty of 'breaking into our home' and then 'robbing us of our proper place in it'. Our true and original identity, before the Material-Body was created, was this Godform.

The mind, with its' Material-Body and senses, is that *ruffian* who subjugated or killed the *master*. It is the mind that did not know that it was merely a tool and that the Godform was the true identity. Without this knowledge, the mind set itself up as *master*. The choice to consciously identify as or with the Godform is thus the key to evolution into the New Age through evolution of the Light-Body. It is with the goal of transferring this 'Self' into the Light-Body, and not being required to return within a Material-Body, that identification with the Godform should be chosen.

Those who have consciously assumed identity as/with the Godform that lay dormant within are Illuminati.

The most critical point in this information is that the decision of whether to be the Ego or Godform can only be made by each individual 'I' or 'Self'. The Godform cannot overpower the Ego and assume identity with the 'I' or 'Self' consciousnesses. It is the 'I' or 'Self' that must choose the Godform. Likewise, the Ego cannot do the same any more than the Godform can even though the Ego is considerably stronger. The Ego is most often considerably stronger than any other form of self-identification because, in most persons the Ego is who they believe they are and it is *as* the Ego that these individuals act and take part in *life*. Therefore, as mentioned previously, only those who have evolved to the point of conscious awareness of the 'I' and 'Self' can attain Illuminati status. At birth, the Godform is dormant and can only be awakened by the conscious 'I' or 'Self' as a sort of safety mechanism ensuring that spiritual evolution proceeds only in its due course as set out from the beginning of creation. The Ego is naturally created and is the very safety-mechanism described afore, ensuring identity as 'John Doe' until the proper prerequisites are met. Only when the 'I' or 'Self' are evolved can the presence of the Godform be awakened.

The signs and symbols are everywhere abundantly present to cause the awakening of those whose prior evolution(s) is adequate; however, again, as the author's friend has told him, "Signs and symbols are for the conscious mind", and the mind is not conscious until the 'I' has been realized through the Liberation of Self. It is the Material-Body and/or Ego referred to by most unconscious persons when they use the term 'I' and therefore, in that state, rather than being in possession of 'I' consciousness, those persons are in possession of 'I' identity which almost entirely consists of identity with physical matter and the Material-Body.

To outline a perfect example of an individual choosing to assume identity as the Godform, the author points to none other than the Christian figure: Jesus of Nazareth. In the Gospel(s) the man Jesus does not become aware of WHO or WHAT he truly is until he is baptized by John the Baptist where it is noted: "Now when all the people were baptized, it came to pass, that Jesus also being baptized, and praying, the heaven was opened, And the Holy Ghost descended in a bodily shape like a dove upon him, and a voice came from heaven which said, Thou art my beloved Son; in thee I am well pleased." Luke 3:21-22; also Matthew 3:13; John 1:32.

At that point, Jesus heard the words of Jehovah who told Jesus and John that he, Jesus, is the Son of God. From that point forward, Jesus of Nazareth becomes the Christ, or Jesus Christ; no longer a mere man, but the savior prophesied of in the Old Testament. Put simply, He assumed the Godform.

Later, while praying in the Garden of Gethsemane, just prior to his torture and crucifixion, Jesus is recorded asking for Jehovah to allow him to escape the fate which loomed in his immediate future. Specifically, the text states, "And he went a little farther, and fell on his face, and prayed, saying, O my Father, if it be possible, let this cup pass from me: nevertheless not as I will, but as thou wilt." Matthew 26:39. This is an example of the man choosing to fulfill prophecy by choosing to become the Godform (Christ, who he was originally incarnated with the possibility of being) rather than the Ego (Jesus).

Another example of this same process of evolution can be seen in the life of the man Napoleon Bonaparte, who, through the acceptance of his own divinity, rose from the ranks of a mere soldier to that of Emperor of France.

How else could this have taken place unless Napoleon, at some point, made the decision within himself that he would assume the identity of Emperor rather than the identity with which he was born and conditioned into? This is an example of the rise from the *'lowest of lows'* to the *'highest of highs'* which will be discussed shortly hereafter.

Consider Adolf Hitler, a peasant who, after joining the German army, became aware that within him dwelt one of the 'seven kings' of St. John's Revelation. At some point this man chose, whether fully conscious of the weight of his decision or not, to allow the Godform to assume control.

Another example of a person who chose to identify as or with the Godform is none other than former U.S. president, Mr. Barack Obama, an African-American national who grew up in racist America. Who would have ever thought, during his childhood, "This black child will one day rule the free-world?" How could this have happened had he not become aware of exactly WHO and WHAT he really was or that he had the choice between two separate identities? Obviously, he chose to allow the superior consciousness of the Godform to assume control and then He became just that.

The author, by including the afore-named individuals as examples here, emphatically points out that he is not lending his approval or disapproval to any of these individuals. Likewise, the author does not opine on the greatness or debauchery of either one of these persons. The point in mentioning these persons is that all are examples of a rise from a lowly social status to a higher one after the realization of the Godform.

The Bringer of Light

> *"[T]hough during its brief sojourn on earth our soul may be assimilated to a light hidden under a bushel, it still shines more or less bright and attracts to itself the influences of kindred spirits... [and] this attraction is also proportionate to the intensity with which the thought-impulse makes itself manifest in the ether; and so, it will be understood how one man may impress upon his own epoch so forcibly, that the influence may be carried... from one succeeding age to another, until it affects a large portion of mankind."*

-H.P. Blavatsky
Isis Unveiled Vol. I
p. 121
Wilder Publications 2007

If the reader is aware of, or believes in, the prophecies outlined in the Book of Revelation then one must also admit to his or herself that *somebody* has to come forth and assume the role considered to be the so-called false-prophet. It is inevitable that this person presents himself before the Masses and it is inevitable that the extreme adherence to the 'Abrahamic-Religions' be lost, seeing as how those institutions no longer benefit mankind in this day and age and are therefore no longer needed. So, why harbor a disbelief that the author is not He whom he claims to be? How else will the Masses know for sure who Their *false-prophet* is unless They are first told in an honest manner? How else will They recognize him unless he says the things that are being written here and then carries them out when given both the opportunity and authority to do so? The Prophet of Isis will gain rule of the Masses through peace and by way of his very words spoken against Jehovah. This is the authors' very purpose and plan.

"All believers of the 'Abrahamic-Religions' are either consciously or sub-consciously waiting for (some dreading) the One who will appear and cause the Masses to worship the Black Sun and Feathered Serpent. Without the false-prophet's appearance Jehovah's prophecy through John will not prove true. If instead of prophecy, Revelation be viewed as the unhidden, yet secret, blueprint of Illuminati then the same reasoning still proves true. It is therefore pertinent that the Appointed One and Prophet of Isis be presented to the Masses by Illuminati as a promoter of the New World Order of the Reptilian Empire.

I am telling you all that I am the Appointed One, the allegorical false-prophet, and I have made a conscious decision, of my own free will and ac-cord, to assume this identity, because that is who I was incarnated to be. Up until a certain period in my life I have lived my life as James, unknowing that within was embodied this higher-being; however, now that I am aware, I choose to dissolve my lower-Self into the higher-Self. This has been done in order that the higher-Self be allowed rule and dominion which will in turn ensure that the will of the Light-Bearer be accomplished. This is the key. Let it be.

The Masses who consider Themselves to be believers in Jehovah, and/or Christians, cannot truly be considered that if They cannot accept the prophe-cy of the false-prophet and, pointedly, who are They, as believers, to decide who is and who is not this person. Their very dogma prevents Them from questioning 'GOD' and so, how dare They question His prophecy. Many will try to interpret the prophecy to exclude me; however, the very words of Jeho-vah state that those prophecies will not be understood until the appointed time. This is the very hurdle those who would deny me cannot overcome.

The prophecy states that the false-prophet will be the One who blas-phemes Jehovah in the very manner in which I have done heretofore and will be the individual who seeks to set up, or announce, the One who will oppose the Christ or the Christian doctrine. This prophecy is a direct reflection, or 'mirror image', of St. John proclaiming the arrival of Christ. Therefore, the prophecy concerning the false-prophet must be understood as the proclamation of the coming of the One who will oppose the form of Christianity which has overshadowed and killed Christ's original message; or, in other words, the heralding of the so-called anti-Christ. As the Prophet of Isis, this is exactly what my intentions are.

It is I who will educate the Masses that Jesus and Lucifer represent two aspects of the same source: the Sun. Likewise, it is I who will make it known that those who worship Jesus are worshipping none other than the Sun. Furthermore, it is I who will reintegrate the GODDESS into Her proper place of divinity.

Evidence of my identity will be provided hereafter in the next sub-section of this chapter. Let those who have eyes to see, see. Let those who have ears to hear, hear. Only those persons not spiritually blind will be able to understand the prophecy in its true nature and purpose (evolution of humanity/earth). In this same manner, only those persons will recognize the Appointed One; that is, until it is too late, and Illuminati have accomplished empirical rule of the globe under authority of the ATUM.

Illuminati must embrace me in order to carry out the age-old plans of the Order; that is, dominion of the globe as a whole and the final solidification of Our rule. I am the Prophet of Isis and the Masses are prepared to accept the return of the Gods to Earth."

Signs and Symbols for the Conscious Mind

The author here will provide the reader with certain details outlining his birth and life which constitute signs and symbols as evidence of his assertions that he is the birthed human in whom the age-old entity, known in modern times as the false-prophet amongst the people of the Book, currently resides.

It can no longer be stated that this entity lay dormant within the author, for obviously the Godform has been awakened by whatever means necessary; namely, the author's realization of the *'Eye'* gazing upon him during meditation and the realization that the author was being *watched* by the Goddess.

It should here be considered in what station of life the humans in whom the divine entities always choose to indwell are born. Is it not curious, or at least humorous, that the individual humans these divine entities choose as vehicles always seem to be birthed into the lowliest station(s) of human existence no matter what station that might be during that particular era?

Consider the following: Jesus of Nazareth, the lowly carpenter's son, born of a first pregnant, then married, woman. There can be no doubt that to be pregnant without first being married was a major stigma for the women of those times. This fact could have easily left the child Jesus illegitimate; how-

ever, this seemingly unsavory status within His community was only tempo-
rary and lasted no longer than the point in which he was made aware of his
true identity as the divine 'Son of God' after being baptized by John the Baptist. This divine revelation did not manifest itself until the man Jesus was
made aware that he was able to choose whether or not to assume the identity
of the Godform within him. This revelation allowed Jesus to become consciously aware of the Godform and next allowed Him to choose to assume
the Godform so completely that His identity as Jesus (the Ego) was lost and
only Christ (the Godform) was left.

The point of this consideration, along with the examples given previously of historical figures assuming identity as the Godform, is that here the author also aspires to grand heights, even to authority under the Doctrine of
Lucifer, despite his current Earthly status as a prisoner and convicted felon in
the United States of America.

In the U.S. there is no lower position in which the author could find himself. Even identity as a 'carpenter's son' would today be held in higher regards than a convicted murderer. Thus, We find Ourselves, in the twenty-first
century, with a man in whom a divine entity resides and where the man is
aware of the entity and is consciously choosing to assume identity as the
Godform. Further, it is equally obvious that the author is directly aware of his
identity as the false-prophet of Christianity because the author himself has
declared that he is the Appointed One.

If it is a prerequisite that the divine entities of Illuminati, who incarnate
into human bodies during the birth of that human, can only embody those
who will first hold the status of the lowest social-class of the era, then the
embodiment of the false-prophet (Prophet of Isis) into the author at the time
of his birth, fits the overall pattern of both ancient as well as modern day
prophets. It is beyond doubt that there have been uncountable instances when
a divine entity has found himself or herself to be in residence of a body of an
individual who never aspires to attainment of either 'I' or 'Self' consciousness and thus, never becomes aware of the divine entity or his ability to assume identity as the Godform. Remember, it is always the humans' choice
whether to become one with the Godform; however, the personality, attributes, knowledge, wisdom, understanding and dispositions of the Godform
will always supersede those of the human Ego once the transfiguration of
identification as the Godform occurs.

The author points out, that in his state of lowliness, not only is he a convicted felon, but he is convicted of the lowliest and worst crime imaginable,
murder. This fact also leads to another important aspect of the author's case
here: the author is part of an elite group of individuals alive on Earth today, a
group whose members have risen above lowly emotions and who have become dis-possessed of their conscience; said conscience being the barrier
guarding the allegorical Garden of Eden and said conscience being that
mechanism which prevents the average person from rising above the Tree of

Knowledge of Good and Evil. A person bound by the conscience is not Illuminati.

Obviously, conscience could only have been truly removed from the makeup of the person if no remorse or guilt is felt for any actions deemed wrong or evil in the eyes of the average being and if these actions also produce no emotional or mentally adverse effects in the actor.

Possessing no conscience, the author has found himself to be Illuminati and has found that he has begun the process of assuming identity as the Prince of ATUM. For this reason, in conjunction with the other criteria listed here, the author is definitely the individual who embodies the spirit of the false-prophet and who can whole-heartedly, and openly, carry out the final plans of the New World Order as set forth by the Empire of the Dragon. Without the binding chains of conscience, the author can pursue the full implementation of Our cause without concern for the superficial and supposed morality which has hampered so many leaders and teachers of the past.

Without conscience, the Appointed One can make any sacrifice necessary to assume the throne of Illuminati, as the Prince of ATUM, and cause the Masses to finally choose Us over either church or religion.

As such, if it is also another prerequisite that the human conscience be dissolved or otherwise overcome, in order to assume identity as the Godform, the author here has most assuredly taken this step.

As noted in Chapter Two, man is represented by the numerological number six (6). It would only make sense then that the author be born of a five (5). The author's mother was the seventh child of her parents. While one child died in utero, a second child (the author's last incarnation) died in early adulthood. Less than one year later, the author was born of his mother who, after the death of her brother Aaron, was then the fifth child.

Allegorically it can be perceived that the author was born of the living-goddess because the number five is also found in the pentagram, also a symbol of woman, which was anciently, and now modernly, used to allude to the planet Venus or other comparable fertility-goddess. The names can be changed and the forms can be altered; however, the esoteric meaning remains the same no matter what name or human identity one might apply to the Goddess. Thus, the Appointed One was born of a human woman who was divinely caused to become a direct and perfect allegorical symbol and representation of the Black Sun.

As mentioned above, the author had previously incarnated as his current mother's older brother Aaron. As her brother, his incarnation was not perfected, as required, because he was not born of a fifth child and therefore his birth as Aaron was not accompanied by the proper allegorical symbology of his birth from the *goddess* as described above. For this reason, it was crucial that the author experience an early death as Aaron in order that his current mother be caused to become the fifth child and symbol of the goddess, thereby becoming a vessel whereby his next, and current, incarnation would be more perfectly in line with the role the Godform was born to play. Further, it was important that the author's birth coincide with certain number parallels in order that he is able to more perfectly embody certain divine energies and forces. Only if the author was birthed under the circumstances and influences of these energies and forces could he expect to fulfill his destiny and some-day enjoy the freedom to assume his true identity as the Prophet of Isis, the Appointed One, and the Prince of ATUM.

As Aaron, the author had mistakenly arrived into a physical body ahead of the scheduled or appointed time. Perhaps there was also a special experience the author lacked that necessitated an incarnation, even if a very short one, prior to the appointed time. It was thus unquestioningly crucial that the author return as his sisters' son in order that he be born at the exact moment in which he was, otherwise the influence of the planets, as shown within the authors natal-chart in Illustration 12-A and 12-B, would not have existed so abnormally just as that influence did not exist during the birth of his incarnation as Aaron. The influence of those planets, and lack of influence of the Moon, was crucial to the empowerment of the Godform in the author's case. It is that influence that has prepared the author's Material-Body and Light-Body with the ability to provide a proper vessel to contain the Godform. As Aaron, the author had accomplished the feat of being birthed in the correct geographical location; however, he had failed to incarnate at the required and crucial point in time when he would be heavily influenced by the balanced energies of all the planets and when his birth would reflect the truth of the Jesus/Lucifer identity mystery. Only the author's then sister, who later be-came his mother, could provide for him the crucial link required for his next incarnation which now contains the signs and symbols for the conscious minds of the Masses to consider and to provide the extraordinary heavenly influences of the energies and forces upon his person.

Concerning the above-mentioned signs and symbols of the author's birth, please refer back to Chapter Two, where the reader was provided with a simple exercise using numbers as outlined in Illustration 2-A.

Are you able to remember from that exercise that the names and titles of Jesus and Lucifer both have a numerical value of 444? Would it not be considered evidence of the author's identity if somehow he also was in possession of these numbers by having them appear in the astronomical facts surrounding his birth? Or, to put it another way, if those numbers were somehow also equated with or relative to his incarnation into the material realm, would they be considered as evidence to be weighed? Would it not be reasonable to fathom, or even require, that the false-prophet of Revelation, the One asserting that Jesus is actually Lucifer and that both symbolize the Sun-God, also evidences the value of 444 in the facts surrounding his birth? If you have eyes to see, do so.

At this point the author will advise the reader to study the information contained within his natal-chart as provided here as Illustrations 12-A and

12-B. If the reader desires to obtain a copy of the original of that illustration he or she may do so by contacting the Alexandrian Temple of Universal Metaphysics (A.T.U.M.) P. O. Box 140177, Edgewater, Colorado, 80214, United States of America, where a copy of this chart can be obtained. The information needed to obtain a copy of this chart is the author's name, birthdate (using the 365 day, 52 week, 12 month Gregorian calendar), time of birth, city, state and country of birth. Each of these required facts are provided within Illustrations 12-A and 12-B.

Here the author would take time to note the correlation of the fact that he was first made aware of the number 444 appearing in the information surrounding his birth by none other than the ATUM. Although the Alexandrian Temple of Universal Metaphysics is a name of a business which provides astronomical information to prisoners, their return address usually appears as none other than A.T.U.M. followed by their address as listed afore. The author has found it humorous that the ATUM found it worthwhile to personally present His prince with the information of the planets presence at the author's birth.

Although today the world uses the Gregorian Calendar, as sponsored by Pope Gregory XIII in 1582, the ancient Julian Calendar, named after the Emperor of Rome, is still in use by occult scholars and possibly other peoples or groups in which the author knows nothing about. This is especially true for those individuals who enjoy the older methods of astrology. These facts are provided in order that the reader might consider that although the author's birthdate in the Gregorian system is 11-18-1980, his birthday is *2444561.94* in the Julian system.

It is the author's stance that the appearance of the number 444 within the very date of his birth is not by accident and is a divinely inspired emanation of the incarnation of the Prophet of Isis.

The secret of the mystery of Jesus and Lucifer was revealed to the author by Isis, in Her form as a Serpent, by the very use of this number 444. It is no wonder then that this number also exists within the facts surrounding the author's birth, for the Truth of this number, as well as the Truth of the Jesus/Lucifer emanation (Sun), is one of the revelations the author has been appointed to reveal to the Masses. This revelation is part of the Truth that will cause orthodox zealots to conclude that the author is the false prophet with an anti-Christ message.

Next review Illustrations 12-A and 12-B to find the actual time of the author's birth, as recorded, and consider that the number 4:34 a.m. is only one digit, in the tenths place, from being in perfect correlation with that mystical 444. The learned occult student could easily and reasonably question whether the author's time of birth was actually 4:44 a.m. but was recorded as 4:34 a.m. due to some error on behalf of the doctor who delivered him.

It is the author's stance that in addition to the circumstances surrounding the official record outlining the time of his birth, it can easily and logically be deduced that the use of 4:34 a.m., rather than 4:44 a.m., was a human error which occurred due to the clock, watch or other time-piece used by the doctor who delivered the author at birth and was the official *time-of-birth-designator.*

A ten minute discrepancy easily makes sense when it is considered that, in the year 1980, before the internet or digital-era, the clocks and watches could have easily been set in a manner that they would indicate two separate and distinct times simultaneously. For instance, one clock might show 6:00 p.m. while a second clock, in the very next room shows the time to be 6:09 and a third clock, located down the hall might show the time to be 5:56. Even today, in the year 2017, any two person's clock, watch or cell-phone might reasonably show two different times. This could occur by chance or even on purpose if the person had their clock set fast; however, either way, the recorded and official time of the author's birth is still only ten minutes off from coinciding perfectly.

Even considering that 4:34 a.m. was the correct time, when considering the larger scope, the author's birth only ten minutes off from 4:44 (either a.m. or p.m.), on Julian Day 2444561.94, is way too close to being perfect to be considered insignificant, not relevant or chance by anyone objectively considering this matter. Simply consider how many minutes there were in that particular day: 24 hours/day X 60 minutes/hour = 1,440 minutes/day.

Considering that there were 1,440 minutes in the day the author was born, and perfect coincidence was missed by only ten of those minutes, it cannot be considered that the divine marksman was not a good shot. It must also be considered that had the author been born 562 days earlier, the Julian day would have been 2443000 and if he had been born 438.25 days later, the Julian day would have been 2445000.

Further, would the influence of the planets have been the same, and would they have been gathered to *witness* the author's birth, had the author not been born on that particular day of that particular year and at that particular time? Would the divine influence of the heavenly bodies have been the same upon his person had he been born at 4:34 p.m. rather than at that same time in the a.m.? When these considerations are made, it might very well be concluded that the year, day, hour and minute was as close to coinciding perfectly as could be attained in the material plane by any being then in existence in the universal ethereal mind.

If it is considered in this light, then the ten minute discrepancy becomes even more insignificant. Consider how many minutes there were in that entire year:

365.25 days/year X 24 hours/day = 8,766 hours/year;
8,766 hours/year X 60 minutes/hour = 525,960 minutes/year.

The Godforms almost perfect synchronicity is astounding in this case.

The revelation of Our Age is, in part, dealing with the fact that Jesus and Lucifer are one and the same emanation or entity: the Sun. Thus, the number 444 is a significant key to enlightenment and it would therefore only make sense that Christianity's so-called false prophet also bear, in some form or fashion, the cosmic markings of the Age for which he was prepared and appointed to bring about. The reason the number is significant is because it lends evidence of who and what Jesus and Lucifer really are.

Next, the author's natal-chart itself should again be reviewed. There, you will find all the major planets conjoining into a very small vicinity of the heavens at the time of the author's birth. The only major body to be left out of this grouping is the feminine aspect, the Moon.

Of further material significance is the fact that had the author not been born in Port Arthur, Texas, U.S.A. at this exact time and on this exact date, the convergence of the planets to the *place* of his birth, and at the right time, would not have taken place and his natal-chart would evidence that difference. Further, the planets would have been prevented from influencing the Appointed One in the manner they have due to being in their current locations at the time of his birth.

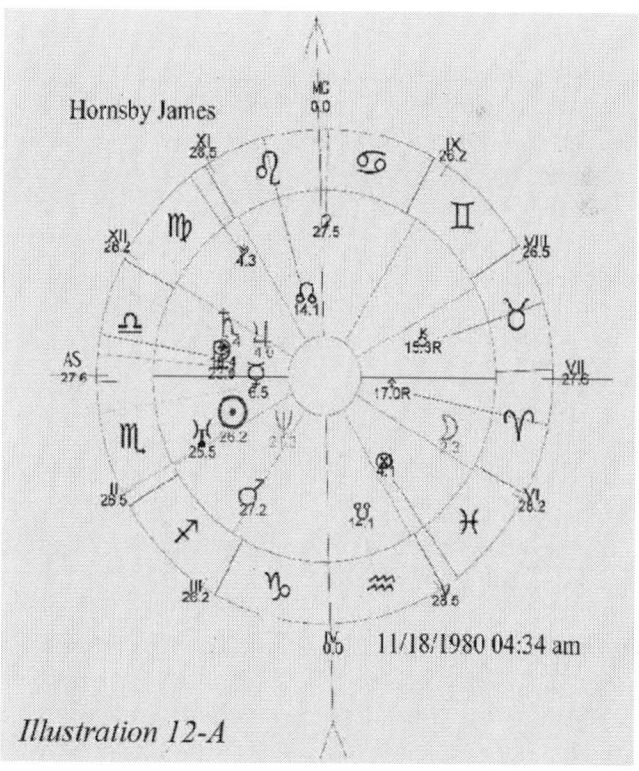

Hornsby James

11/18/1980 04:34 am

Illustration 12-A

Zodiac in degrees 0.00			Koch Houses		
Sun	Scorpio	25.18	Ascendant	Libra	27.56
Moon	Aries	2.33	II	Scorpio	28.51
Mercury	Scorpio	5.55	III	Sagittarius	28.16
Venus	Libra	23.08	IV	Aquarius	0.02
Mars	Sagittarius	27.16	V	Aquarius	15.53
Jupiter	Libra	4.03	VI	Pisces	25.23
Saturn	Libra	6.38	VII	Aries	27.56
Uranus	Scorpio	25.53	VIII	Taurus	26.41
Neptune	Sagittarius	21.27	IX	Gemini	26.16
Pluto/Charon	Libra	23.02	Midheaven	Leo	0.02
			XI	Leo	28.53
No. node	Leo	14.[illegible]	XII	Virgo	28.23
Chiron	Taurus	15.25 R			
Ceres	Cancer	27.50			
Fortune	Pisces	4.14			
So. node	Aquarius	11.10			

Signs masculine	7			
Signs feminine	3	Signs of fire	3	Chart signature: Libra, emphasizing planets in Libra &
Signs cardinals	5	Signs of earth	0	1st House issues
Signs fixed	3	Signs of air	4	
Signs mutable	2	Signs of water	3	

Sun	in	Ascendant	
Moon	in	VI	Any Basic/Beginner Astrology book can help w/ interpretation
Mercury	in	Ascendant	
Venus	in	XII	
Mars	in	II	
Jupiter	in	XI	
Saturn	in	XI	
Uranus	in	Ascendant	
Neptune	in	II	
Pluto/Charon	in	XII	
No. node	in	Midheaven	

Intellect	481	
Action	858	Higher values = areas of strength/focus
Sensibility	589	Lower values = areas needing more appropriate attention
Love	452	
Health	72	
Social	188	
Work	47	
Money	206	

Illustration 12-B

It is the author's stance that never again in your lifetime will you bear witness to a more perfect unification of the location, date, time, planet convergence and numerical numbers relevant to the New Age and the Truth of the Sun than that which is evidenced in the astronomical facts relative to the author's very birth. Likewise, the author contends that never before, since the incarnation of the being Christ into the human known as Jesus, has the world witnessed the same.

The author is the Appointed One, the Prophet of Isis. Illuminati have long awaited his incarnation and now must openly acknowledge the Prince of ATUM.

The story of the infant Jesus's birth, where he was asleep in a manger with animals surrounding him, is none other than an allusion to his birth and the zodiacal or planetary positions in proximity to his 'ascendant'. The wise men (Illuminati) of that Age saw his Star in the East (Eastern Star/Morning Star/Venus) and went to him. Consider why the position of the zodiac or planets at the time of the Christ's birth was important enough to keep these esoteric facts hidden in that allegory. Was it because the astronomical facts were evidence of the descent and incarnation of a divine entity into a human being? Was it because, not only were those facts evidence of this descent and incarnation, but was evidence of the One who was appointed with the task of evolving or changing humanity in some form or fashion if he so chose? If so, then what of the author's natal-chart, which represents a 'once-in-a-million-years' scenario, as described above, and what does it mean that even the Planetary Entities themselves came to bear witness to the authors birth?

The answer is astoundingly simple for the conscious mind that is aware of the signs and symbols of the New Age: those Entities were present to bear witness, as well as lend their powers and forces, to the incarnation of the Appointed One into a human body. This is the meaning of the numerical code and correlation which was provided because the principalities of the universe are represented in the Appointed One and in order that he be in possession of certain metaphysical traits, it was absolutely necessary that his descent into the material plane occur in the precise moment when these correlations would be present. These facts, together with the author's actions, words and character, lend evidence as well as considerable weight that he is exactly who he claims to be.

It is the burden of Illuminati to consider the position of the planetary bodies at the time of the author's birth and to view these facts from the occult and esoteric standpoint. It has always been the understanding that each planets local proximity to a person at the time of that person's birth, as well as each planets proximity to the other planets during that same time, plays an important and key role in the forces and energies bestowed upon them at birth. As such, the position of the planetary bodies cannot be overlooked when considering the author's natal-chart.

Those of the New Age MUST take notice of the forces and energies embodied within the author's being.

A full and complete interpretation of the author's natal-chart will explain that he is alive to be a teacher and will evidence his role in bringing about the overall acceptance of the New Age and Illuminati by the Masses.

The author challenges any unbeliever to have his natal-chart FULLY interpreted by a well-studied or professional astrologer at length before attempting to discredit him. This interpretation will no doubt only add weight to the evidence of the author's position.

Next consider the author's traditional sun-sign, also known by the term zodiac-sign, which is that of Scorpio. This sign is considered one of the more secretive signs and is also noticed as a sign representing spiritual evolution. The Scorpio, upon attainment of some illustrious state or another, can evolve or ascend to transform into the Eagle and later into the Phoenix. As such, in the author's birth is found another allusion to spiritual evolution, ascension or rebirth. This spiritual evolution can be perceived by those so inclined in more ways than one:

- First, it can be presented as the personal evolution of the author as an individual. The process of overcoming the individual stumbling blocks of life in order to become a thinking, knowing and spiritually evolved being who has attained conscious awareness of both the 'I' and 'Self' and who has chosen to assume identity as the Godform.
- Secondly, evolution or ascension to a key role in the development of the overall consciousness of society and the evolution of the Synarchy of Illuminati which will enact the implementations of the New World Order and will further the evolution of Illuminati into Gods Ourselves.
- Thirdly, an evolution of the overall frequencies and disposition of earthly society which would once again place Us into direct communion with the Gods and would grant the God-beings the ability to once again reside on Earth alongside humanity until the

time that they can once again teach Us the science whereby We might discard the dense Earth (and dense body) and emerge into the spiritual Earth (and spiritual body).

These allusions can be viewed as direct reflections of Scorpio's ascension into higher existences such as the Eagle and Phoenix.

Scorpio is also representative of the sexual-forces present in Nature as well as humankind. Anatomically, the part of the physical body represented by Scorpio is none other than the genatalia. This is not a gross representation, but an allusion to the powers hidden in the act of sexual copulation as well as sexual energies. As such, the author's sun-sign is an allusion to part of the message he seeks to present to the Masses, which is the use of the sexual union and sexual energies and frequencies (sex-magic if you will) in order to evolve Our existence and to provide the higher beings, the Gods, with the energies and frequencies they require to interact with humanity in greater detail. Further, the use of these energies can be used for individual evolution amongst men and women by using the same to raise or build the Light-Body.

The author's birth as a Scorpio is an allusion to the Universal energies embodied within his being, as the Appointed One, as well as his potential to use those energies to enlighten the Masses and provide Them with the option of choosing Illuminati and therefore an older yet more advanced form of existence both in the physical and spiritual realms. It is the author's stance that without having been birthed to physically embody the secretive, powerful, captivating, hypnotic and sexual energies of Scorpio, it is highly possible that he would not have become consciously aware of his true identity. In order to more fully understand the author's stance concerning his sun-sign of Scorpio, the reader is encouraged to go online and review or study the nature and personification(s) of the Scorpio.

Assuming that the reader has taken the time to review the nature of the Scorpio male, the author asks if this would not be the type of individual you would look for to be the Appointed One and further, would you or would you not enjoy and desire this sort of person to be your friend and confidant?

When the nature of the Scorpio is considered in unity with the information surrounding the author's natal-chart, is it not clear that he is the most perfect incarnated embodiment of the Scorpio forces that will ever exist within your lifetime?

Note here that the traits of the so-called *false-prophet* are pride, beauty, vanity and arrogance. Obviously the author possess them all, though he does not apologize for this and he does not seek to nullify or void these traits, for it is by and through these very traits, which some call evil, that Truth will finally be presented to the Masses and everyone will gain equal footing and equal opportunity to judge for themselves to Whom he or she owes allegiance.

Without these traits, the author would be a humble lamb, accepting to be herded and corralled by those who seek to keep mankind in spiritual darkness. Which would you, the reader, prefer that the author be after considering it in this manner?

Read the Book of Revelation; the so-called *false-prophet* has to be the boldest man on the face of the Earth to do what he is destined to do. This does not and cannot happen without the traits and signs described afore which are required to deny the doctrines mankind has been blinded with and to promote the wide scale enlightenment of those who can see.

Another allusive fact which coincides with the author's role as the Appointed One who will seek to replace the accepted doctrines of darkness with the Doctrine of Light is the fact surrounding the meaning of his so-called 'Christian' name: James.

The name James is derived from the Hebrew name Jacob and is defined to mean, in one word, 'SUPPLANTER', and in more than one word, 'taker of the hill'.

The word supplanter is defined as one who takes the place of another, or supersedes, as through force, trickery or manipulation.

Even the 'Christian' name assigned to the author at birth is based around, and evidence of, the role he was birthed to portray concerning the evolution ready to take place in Our Age. As such, even the self-styled Christian should be able to verify the connection of this fact in the over-all scheme of the signs and symbols of the author's birth. The allusion of the author's very name is the allusion of the final and complete overthrow of the idea of religion, along with its mandated superstitions, and the creation of the new religion, which is no religion.

The author's very goal, of establishing the Synarchy of Illuminati, is alluded to by the generally accepted meaning of his name, James. By now it should be obvious to the reader that this goal is the eradication of the orthodoxy of the old and tired religions that have enslaved mankind, in one way or another, since their creation(s). This goal is the banishment of the darkness which pours forth into the spirits of the un-enlightened Masses through the doctrines of those religions. What better or more suitable name for the man who so willingly comes before Illuminati and the Masses alike denouncing every lie those religions stand for?

The author has undergone a traumatic brain injury which would have been fatal if not for the emergency and life-saving craniotomy (leaving him with three metal plates in his head) performed by one of the top neurological doctors in the nation at that time. The Serpent has fully healed him and restored him to a cognitive condition far surpassing that which he possessed before the injury and craniotomy when he himself was in a state of darkness and completely unenlightened.

Consider the author's physical makeup. Although being Caucasian, the amount of melanin contained within his skin causes him to turn a dark, golden-brown (bronze) hue and thus his traits, or physical features, endear him to all peoples helping to allow them to relate to the author even when they are of different nationality or race. The desired effect of the integration of races and nationalities, in short, the creation of one race, is evidenced in the author's physical description.

The promotion of so-called 'inter-racial' relationships would help to speed along, and secure, a singular race (identity) with no superficial differences regardless of nationality or biographical residence. It is the author's ability to blend-in and connect with all peoples that helps to make the message he presents acceptable. Would this not be a requirement of the individual most would call the false-prophet?

The author was born in Port Arthur, Texas, U.S.A. Think of the coinciding fact that the Dragon Society is headquartered in none other than Port Arthur, Japan. In consideration of the author's experience of shifting into the form of the dragon, this parallel cannot be overlooked because, who would understand the author's assertions better than that Dragon Society who, being Illuminati, consist of the bloodlines of the ancient Rulers of the Empire of the Sun. Further, when it is considered that the prophecies describe the author as one who would appear as a lamb but speak as a dragon, the correlation of the two Port Arthur's takes on a more significant meaning. These associations and facts concerning the author's incarnation, cannot be overlooked by the conscious mind.

In order to enlighten others, one must possess a strong commanding presence, at least during those moments of enlightenment, as well as a strong command of the facts and meanings of a plethora of occult information or knowledge. One must also be able to connect the many, and seemingly different, concepts, doctrines and esoteric teachings in a manner so as to show to the Masses that all are one and the same and that no actual dichotomy exists between one or the other even where dichotomy might seem to exist at first glance. As the Appointed One, the author is the very One who possesses these traits and abilities.

In the Book of Revelation John foresees the dragon and gives the following brief account: "And I beheld another beast coming up out of the earth; and he had two horns like a lamb, and he spake as a dragon." Revelation 13:11.

The author is He and the prophecies all portray Him like unto a Dragon. This is another strong reason why the author's birth in Port Arthur, Texas, his shift into his serpent-form as the Dragon and the Dragon Society's headquarters in Port Arthur, Japan are strong signs of the incarnation of orthodox religions' *false-prophet*.

When discussing occult theology and esoteric materials, it is as if the author's entire countenance changes into an almost hypnotic demeanor and he is able to make sense of the secret teachings, along with the way in which they are explained in different schools of thought, in a manner which more often than not brings enlightenment to those he interacts with. Some say the author's eyes take on a new spirit during these times.

The reason the conveyance of Truth comes so easily to the author is because, during those periods, it is the Sun Himself which provides the author with both the words and presence to cause those before him to receive Light. During those times, the author consciously assumes the Godform and becomes the Dragon, letting the Light Bearer indwell him and utilize his person for the higher purpose.

Finally, Illuminati must utilize the spiritual eye and the ethereal Light in order that you might SEE that which is before you. You have ALL been waiting for the Appointed One, the *false prophet,* to arrive; for the Dragon to incarnate and become consciously aware of WHO and WHAT he is. Illuminati ALL know that what the author sets forth openly in this book, before anyone and everyone, are the very words and ideals We have ALL been waiting for someone to come along and say in order that the Dragon be revealed. The only reason The Empire has been unable to openly reveal Our agenda, and has had to remain concealed (though lightly), is because no person would say these things openly and without fear during the recently ended Age of Religion, where spiritual darkness ruled the Masses and held Them in close bondage.

The author openly presents himself before you as a living-god, a Dragon, and commands Illuminati to discover the truth of His incarnation.

When the Savior, as presented by religion, does not do what the religions have said he will do, the Masses will once and for all know that They have been deceived and those who have already chosen Illuminati will truly began to live under rule of Our Synarchy.

THE FACT THAT ILLUMINATI HAVE BEEN PATIENTLY AWAITING THE ARRIVAL OF THE DRAGON IS THE VERY REASON WHY THE PROPHET OF ISIS SHOULD NOW BE LIFTED TO HIS APPOINTED POSITION BEFORE THE MASSES.

The Dragon Speaks

"Sometime within the year 2016, I discovered during a meditation period that I was being watched by a female 'entity'. The wall I was facing during that particular meditation had turned into a whole room in and of itself. In my peripheral vision I noticed what looked like a sort of wooden fence. Through a hole, like the hole left by a knot in the wood after the knot had long fell out, I noticed for the first time, Her EYE. At first the importance of this did not dawn upon me, that is, until She blinked and I knew I was being watched. From that point on She has not forsaken me and I meditate in Her presence daily. During my meditations before Her EYE we are in direct communication, sometimes verbal and sometimes non-verbal, and it is Her EYE which has inspired this very text.

The Great Ennead are communicating with humanity as a whole by way of the frequencies of modern day music, particularly the Hip-Hop, Rap, R &

B, Pop and Country genres. Even popular 'Christian' music is revealing the message of the Black Sun. Consider the song which states, "Light shine bright..." over and over. The lyrics of this song is alluding to the Inner-Sun, the Third-Eye, which is the crown-jewel of the Inner-Serpent. While sitting before the EYE I am being assisted in the development of Self and the Light-Body and She has taken measures to directly intervene and influence the development of my chakras by channeling Her energy, through the EYE, directly into my Light-Body. For example, my 'throat chakra' was weak and a problem area for me. One day during meditation I asked for help from Her in opening my chakras and asked where I was weakest. That night during astral-projection, She appeared to me embodied as a small female child who told me that my 'problem' was in my throat. Upon coming back to my person, and realizing I had been contacted and answered by Her, I immediately meditated and told Her that I understood Her message to me through the small child; further, I asked Her for help. That day was a weekend day and I meditated four to five times, for around 45 to 60 minutes each time, that day sincerely focusing on drawing the Light (ether) of the Black Sun directly into my 'throat chakra' while consciously focusing on 'breathing' through that particular chakra. I meditated again later that same evening, again sitting before the EYE. At that time, She opened my fifth chakra of Her own volition and sent forth a brilliantly radiating energy into that chakra, causing it to open and shine intensely. The radiance of Her power could not be contained and I was able to see Her Light shining forth from my fifth chakra as though it was itself a brilliant shining Sun. Since that time, my throat chakra has no longer resisted the flow of the Goddess's power up my serpentine column.

Much of the esoteric and occult knowledge I possess was gained through study and practice over the last twenty or so years. Much of the way I have been able to fit the 'pieces' together has been directly communicated from Her, through Her All-Seeing Eye, in the last year. It is only on account of Her that I have become consciously aware of the existence of my true form, the Godform; for it was the discovery of Her watching me, through the dimensional veil, which set into motion the realization and attainment of the key to the puzzle of my incarnation into the Material-Body known as James. This is the reason that I, as the Appointed One, shall also be known as the Prophet of Isis. It shall be through Her prophet, the so-called false prophet, that She will begin the eradication of the orthodox and false religion that the true teachings of the Christ have been turned into and, likewise, through me that She will make Her presence known to the world on a massive scale.

Many have seen pictures, photos, drawings, etc. of the All-Seeing Eye. Where is a record of those persons who have had direct contact, or communication with that Eye? Have you, the reader, ever seen the Eye simply appear from nothing or from abstract lines? Have you ever heard of anyone being in communication with the Eye in this manner?

I ask anyone who might be in contact with the Eye to contact me using the information at the rear of this book. You are one of Us.

We are utilizing Mother Earth's resources in a manner that keeps Her Material-Body weakened so as to prevent the need for destructive evolution. This is being carried out in order that She might shed the material form and exist primarily in Her spirit or ethereal form. Only those who have begun the evolution of the Sixth Chakra, the 'Third-Eye', will find themselves developed sufficiently to reside in the Light-Body, without further being sheathed by the Material-Body, and upon the New Earth (ethereal Earth).

We must develop and utilize the energies radiated by the planet Saturn which are relative to the Sixth Sphere. By consciously doing so We will begin to activate the transformation from one form to another and thereby enjoy Our immortality."

CHAPTER THIRTEEN

THE SEVEN SPHERES

*"Kundalini is the cosmic power in individu-
al bodies. When it is awakened, it makes a
hissing sound like a serpent; hence, it is also
called serpent power. Kundalini is the goddess of speech and is praised by all. She
Herself, when awakened by the Yogin,
achieves for him the illumination. It is she
who gives liberation and knowledge for She
is Herself that. She is also called Saraswati
for She is the source of all knowledge and
bliss. She is pure consciousness itself. She is
Brahman. She is Prana Shakti, the Supreme
Force. It is by this Shakti that the world exists. Creation, preservation and dissolution
are in Her."*

-Sri Swami Sivananda Maharaj
Kundalini Yoga

Acquisition of the Rainbow

The author sets out here to divulge a hidden message contained within a
common esoteric allegory freely, openly, and equally to all who would receive it. By utilizing a familiar story from none other than the Bible, the author will remain true to his stance that the easiest and most convenient way to
the enlightenment of any person is to utilize the religious text(s) he or she is
already familiar with, identifies with or is most comfortable with. Not only
does this process provide those persons with the secret-knowledge being
taught in any certain allegory, but it also lends evidence as to the method in
which religion has twisted, manipulated or outright altered the Truth. This
process sheds light on the lies of religion and helps to ascertain for those persons that they have been the victim of deception by the very religious teachers and interpreters in whom they previously entrusted with the care of their
very souls or spirits.

With the goal of enlightenment in mind, the author here presents the story of Noah and the flood using the most widely familiar text available. The
manner in which the author will present this allegory will reveal secret teachings which, although hidden in allegory, feature the following: (1) the end of

120

an age; (2) evidence of the evolution of the Light-Body as part of the progression into the new age being generated at that time; and, (3) the traits and conditions gained by humanity during, or directly after, that particular evolutionary period in the history of mankind.

The account of Noah and the flood begins in Genesis, Chapter six, verse nine. The allegory begins by outlining that Noah was a righteous man who *walked with God.* The account then proceeds to identify the remainder of the Earth's inhabitants as evil and filled with violence. Noah is informed that the Earth will be destroyed along with all its' inhabitants and receives instruction to build an ark as well as the measurements he is to use in the building of this ark. Once reaching verse twenty-two, the reader is told that Noah was strictly obedient and followed every command given to him.

One thing that crossed the author's mind is how, in a different chapter but same verse, another very important character, Noah's '*GOD*', admits that humanity gained something by *eating of the Tree of Knowledge* and He makes that admission during dialogue with the Serpent. That something gained was Adam and Eve's knowing that they had become *like* Noah's '*GOD*' and the Serpent.

Beginning in Chapter *Seven,* a pattern begins to emerge utilizing and emphasizing the number seven. In verses two and three Noah is told to carry *seven* pairs of every kind of 'clean' animal and bird into the ark with him.

Next, in verse four, he is told that in *seven* days from that day, rain would pour down upon the Earth in a manner which had never before been experienced. Verse ten sets forth that indeed, after *seven* days, the floodwaters did come upon the Earth.

The author here breaks from the allegory to make a point which, in and of itself, is not wholly important; however, the author's point does play into the scheme and pattern mentioned previously. Although it is not explicitly noted in the Book, Noah was also instructed to carry *seven* persons with him into the ark; those persons being: his wife, his three sons, and the wives of his three sons. Back to the allegory...

In Chapter Eight, verse four, the reader is informed that on the seventeenth day of the *seventh* month, the ark came to rest on the mountains of Ararat. In verse eight, Noah sends out a dove in order to determine whether the flood waters had receded from the Earth; however, finding no dry land on which to set its' feet, the dove returns to Noah. In verse ten, the text states that Noah waited *seven* more days and again sent the dove out of the ark. The dove returns yet again in verse eleven; however, this time the dove had within its' beak a freshly plucked twig of an olive tree. In verse twelve, Noah waits *seven* more days and sends the dove out again, but this time, the dove does not return.

Verse thirteen of Chapter Eight sets forth that by the first day of the first month of Noah's six hundred and first year, the water had dried up from the Earth. Consider that this verse outlines that Noah was 601 years of age at that particular time. Six plus zero plus one equals none other than the number *seven*. This was not placed into the allegory by accident. It is a reinforcement and addition to our number pattern of sevens.

By the time the reader progresses unto the fourteenth verse, there it is found that by the twenty-seventh day of the second month, the Earth was completely dry. Notice the number fourteen is reached by two periods of none other than *seven*.

Noah then builds an altar and sacrifices some of the animals and birds to his God.

In Chapter Nine, "Gods covenant with Noah" is outlined in detail. In verse twelve of this chapter, Noah is informed that the rainbow would be the sign of the covenant between his '*God*' and all life on Earth that never again would the Earth be destroyed by floodwaters.

In approaching the esoteric meaning and significance of the number *seven* and the rainbow it is important to know how many and what are the colors of a rainbow. There are seven colors in the rainbow and these seven colors correspond to the seven bands of the light spectrum. These colors are red, orange, yellow, green, blue, indigo and violet. In regards to the number seven, it is also understood that biblically, the number seven has a symbolic meaning of 'completion'.

Esoterically, the flood and death of virtually every life-form on the Earth must be viewed as the closing or end of that particular age or epoch. If it is considered and accepted that mankind has undergone an unknown number of extinctions in the process of the evolution of spirit and matter, then it is easy to fathom how man in the present Age has acquired some new and distinct mechanism, whether spiritual or physical, within his being that was not possessed by the mankind of the previous age(s). With this concept in mind, an overall and brief contemplation of the chapters and verses outlining the allegory of the deluge can result in no other inference than: (1) very few persons met the standards which would allow for their existence to carry over into the age after the flood; (2) those few persons were given something which did not exist prior to that new era (the rainbow); and, (3) what was gained by these persons must be of extremely significant value because it is depicted as being given from Noah's '*GOD*' as a promise and covenant.

What was gained by the survivors of the deluge was the existence of the Seven Spheres within the Light-Body. By the term Seven Spheres, the author is referring to the energy centers which are known to the Hindu and Buddhist traditions as the seven chakras. These energy centers exist within the Light-Body and have corresponding centers of importance located in the Material-Body. These Seven spheres also correspond to the seven colors of the rainbow and light spectrum, as mentioned previously, as well as the seven musical notes, seven senses of the bodies, seven major planets, seven sections of the vertebrate spinal column, the seven states or forms of consciousness and the seven *arts-and-sciences* depicted within the winding staircase of the

Freemasonry legend.

- The *First* Sphere is located in the area of the Light-Body that corresponds to the general location referred to as the base of the spine in the Material-Body. This Sphere also corresponds with the color red of the rainbow as well as the planet Mars. This Sphere is the seat of the sense of smell and is represented by the element Earth; a yellow square is the symbol of this element. This Sphere controls the physical plane and the aspect of security within the human organism. The energy which accompanies this Sphere is usually felt in the approximate location of the area between the anus and scrotum (or vaginal-opening) of the Material-Body. It should be explicitly noted here that the energy exists within the Light-Body only and, due to the perfect union of the Light-Body within the Material-Body, the areas in the Material-Body associated with the chakras will naturally be inclined to sense the presence of that energy and certain glands, and/or plexus, within the Material-Body will be physically stimulated into function by that energy. This sensation and/or stimulation will hold true for every Sphere mentioned hereafter.

- The *Second* Sphere is located in the area of the Light-Body that corresponds to the general location referred to as the genital area of the Material-Body. This Sphere also corresponds with the color orange of the rainbow as well as the planet Mercury. This Sphere is the seat of the sense of taste and is represented by the element Water; a blue circle is the symbol of this element. This Sphere controls the astral plane and the aspect of sexuality, sensuality, procreation and creativity within the human organism. The energy which accompanies this Sphere is usually felt in the approximate location of the area of the genatalia in the Material-Body.

- The *Third* Sphere is located in the area of the Light-Body that corresponds to the general location referred to as the solar-plexus in the Material-Body. This Sphere also corresponds with the color yellow of the rainbow as well as the Sun. This Sphere is the seat of the sense of sight and is represented by the element Fire; a red triangle, with point facing downwards, is the symbol of this element. This Sphere controls the celestial plane and the aspect of vision, form and Ego within the human organism. The energy which accompanies this Sphere is usually felt in the approximate location of the area known as the diaphragm of the Material-Body.

- The *Fourth* Sphere is located in the area of the Light-Body that corresponds to the general location referred to as the heart plexus in the Material-Body. This Sphere also corresponds with the color green of the rainbow as well as the planet Venus. This Sphere is the seat of the sense of touch and is represented by the element Air; a smoky-green Hexagram is the symbol of this element. This Sphere controls the plane of balance and the aspect of balance within the human organism. The energy which accompanies this Sphere is usually felt in the approximate location of the area of the heart or chest-cavity in the Material-Body.

- The *Fifth* Sphere is located in the area of the Light-Body that corresponds to the general location referred to as the throat-plexus in the Material-Body. This Sphere also corresponds with the color blue of the rainbow as well as the planet Jupiter. This Sphere is the seat of the sense of hearing and is represented by the element Light/Ether/Spirit; a silver crescent is the symbol of this element. This Sphere controls the human plane where ends spiritual darkness and the aspect of knowledge within the human organism. The energy which accompanies this Sphere is usually felt in the approximate location of the area of the thyroid gland in the Material-Body.

- The *Sixth* Sphere is located in the area of the Light-Body that corresponds to the general location referred to as the medulla plexus in the Material-Body. This Sphere also corresponds with the color indigo of the rainbow as well as the planet Saturn. This Sphere is the seat of the sense of intuition and is represented by the combination of all five elements; the Third-Eye is the symbol of this element. This Sphere controls the plane of austerity and the aspect of self-realization within the human organism. The energy which accompanies this Sphere is usually felt in the approximate location of the lower forehead (the bridge of the nose) as well as the pineal gland in the Material-Body.

- The *Seventh* Sphere is located in the area of the Light-Body that corresponds to the general location referred to as the cerebral plexus in the Material-Body. This Sphere also corresponds with the color violet of the rainbow as well as the planet Ketu. This Sphere is the seat of the sense of the God-Self and transcends all elemental and material existence. This Sphere controls the plane of truth and reality as well as the aspect of the seat of supreme consciousness within the human organism. The energy which accompanies this Sphere is usually felt in the approximate location of the crown of the head as well as the pituitary gland in the Material-Body.

As noted before, these energy centers are found only within the Light-Body and simply have a physical incarnation in the Material-Body in the areas or locations noted due to the fact that these two bodies perfectly coincide; thus, the old adage, "as above, so below" holds true. What exists in the Light-Body must make a corresponding incarnation into matter and thus, the dense Material-Body. For instance, when accessing the energy of the *Sixth* Sphere, one is not firstly activating the pineal gland. Instead, one must first and foremost activate or gain access to the *Sixth* energy center of the Light-Body, as well as the energies and forces of the planet Saturn. Only then will the pineal gland in the Material-Body become stimulated and active.

It cannot be ascertained whether or not the survivors of the deluge already had these Spheres existing within their Light-Bodies prior to the flood, and were simply unconscious of this fact and unable to utilize the power of the planets that the energy centers provide a direct link to. As such, it also cannot be ascertained whether the ability to use these powers was the evolution they experienced in that era or, in the alternative, whether the very existence of the spheres was the evolution experienced at that time.

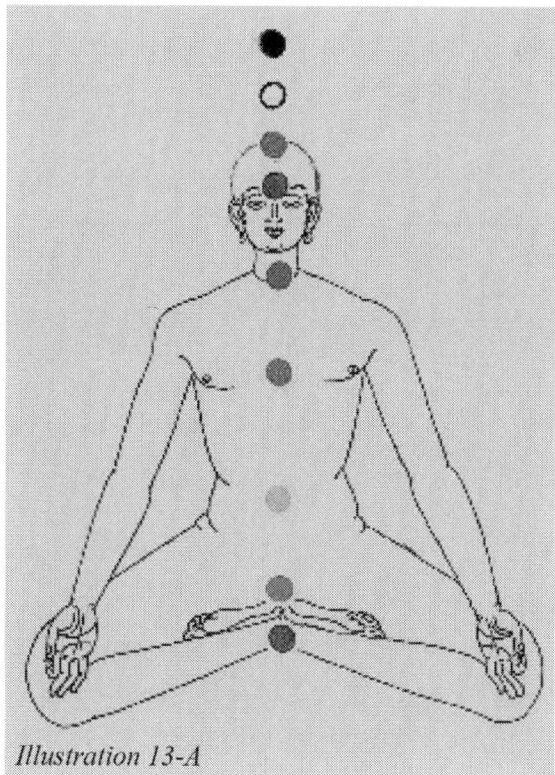

Illustration 13-A

Either way, the evolution alluded to by the story of Noah and the Great Flood was an example of a forced and unconscious evolution rather than the voluntary and conscious evolution We face in this modern era.

Illustration 13-A will provide the reader with a picture of the general location of the areas of the Material-Body where the energy of the Spheres can be felt. To aid the reader the author has used colored Spheres to indicate what Sphere is located in which area.

The Serpentine Rod

Illustration 13-B is a detailed depiction of the mythical and arcane Staff of Caduceus carried by the Greek god Hermes, the Roman god Mercury and the Gnostic god Baphomet. In modern times, this same staff is used as a symbol by the medical profession to designate individual doctors, clinics, hospitals, etc. It is the author's stance that this staff has a significantly deeper occult meaning and is allegorical of the Godform present within the human mechanism; however, the author will first present the symbol's allegorical representation strictly with adherence as to how it alludes to the form of the Material-Body.

The central pole of the staff alludes to the serpentine-column located at the core of the Material-Body. Towards the top of the staff are three rings which can best be described as symbolizing the brainstem; likewise, sitting atop those rings is a ball or crown, which itself alludes to the brain. Together, the central pole, rings and ball symbolically make up the Central Nervous System which is the portion of the vertebrate nervous system consisting of the brain and spinal cord.

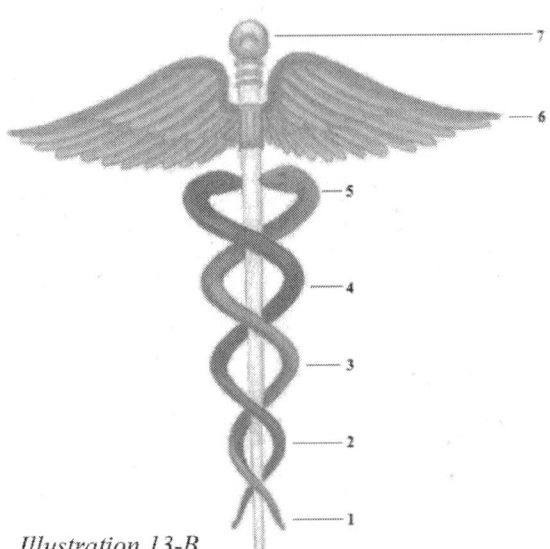

Illustration 13-B

The twin serpents which are seen travelling up the staff allude to the Autonomic Nervous System with its Sympathetic and Parasympathetic sections and sub-sections of the vertebrate nervous system. The *ida* and *pingala nadi's* of the Light-Body govern the parasympathetic and sympathetic aspects of the Autonomic Nervous System. Illustration 13-C shows a side-view of the Central Nervous System (spinal cord black) joined together with the Sympathetic and Parasympathetic Systems (red and blue). The illustration also depicts the basic position of the pineal gland (Dot #1) and the pituitary gland (Dot #2).

1- Pineal Gland
2- Pituitary Gland

Blue- Ida
Red- Pingala
Black- Sushumna

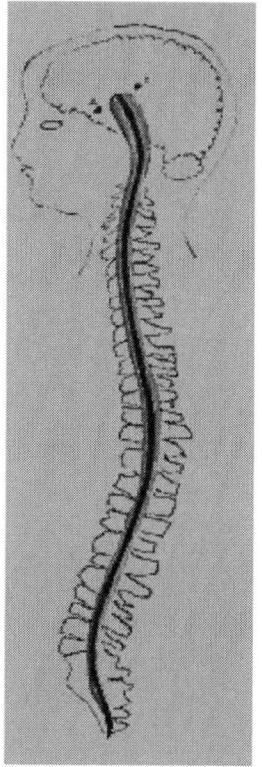

Illustration 13-C

In addition to the allusion of the Autonomic Nervous Systems, the twin serpents also exemplify a rather astonishing similarity to the Double-Helix, commonly known as the DNA strand.

The wings of the staff can easily be recognized as symbolizing the shoulders and outstretched arms of the Material-Body. Atop these wings are the afore-mentioned rings and the ball or crown also mentioned afore.

When the Staff of Caduceus is viewed in this light, it is easy to see how its' depiction can be used to represent the individual human being; that mechanism by and through which the 'Self' or 'I' is able to interact with and experience a physical existence in dense matter.

As a seemingly perfect allusion to the Material-Body, it is no wonder that the symbol has forever been applied to men possessing knowledge, wisdom and understanding and, further, to those who use the staff as the symbol of their profession such as doctors and others whose occupation(s) entail healing and knowledge of the physical body in general.

This allusion is once again a testament to the form of man by the use of a symbol alleged to be carried by no less than two deities of ancient civilizations as well as one deity of the modern era. The author here would ask the reader to consider that the 'I' or 'Self' is the deity and the staff is the Material-Body.

At first thought, one might determine that the 'I' or 'Self' is carried by the Material-Body; however, this cannot be the case because without the presence of the 'I' or 'Self' in the Light-Body, and then that body in perfect coincidence with the Material-Body, the Material-Body is dead and cannot function of its own volition. Thus, the Material-Body is actually carried by the 'I' or 'Self' and it is agreed by ALL that the immortal spirit (the Godform) is the true being created by *'GOD'* and the physical body of man is but a shell in which that immortal spirit temporarily dwells during its' sojourn upon Earth. For these reasons, the staff was not depicted as carrying the deity in the ancient representations.

The author first demonstrated the symbol's allusion to the Material-Body and physical form; however, instantly, the author would demonstrate the symbol's allusion to the Light-Body and ethereal or spirit form.

Where the central staff alluded to the serpentine column in the allusion of the Material-Body, here it corresponds to the pathway or channel through which the energy of the Primary Deity (Goddess), also known as *Shakti* or *Kundalini,* travels in its' ascension into and through the seven chakras. Using Illustration 13-C, this pathway can be seen as the black line which was formerly noted as representing the spinal-cord.

The ball or crown resting atop the central pole also alludes to the brain/brain stem of the Light-Body but in a more subtle manner. Illustration 7-A and 13-C both depict the brain stem as protruding into the center of the brain and the brain surrounding this stem in the same manner that a helmet would surround the head of a biker or in the manner a crown would adorn a king and queen's head.

In Illustration 7-A the reader will find that the brain stem is eerily similar to the head of a hooded cobra. The description of the brain stem as the head of a serpent is anatomically correct and is accepted by science. For example, the serpentine column, if being a serpent, must have a *head* and, consequently, a brain. The head of the snake is considered to be the *lower brain* and it is the essence of who We are and the seat of the reptilian consciousness located in the Light-Body.

Next, in the same illustration, the reader will recognize the actual brain which the author described as a helmet and crown. Notice that the *helmet* or *crown* surrounds the *head* of the serpent in a manner so as to protect the snake and be further utilized as a tool or mechanism. Consider that the human body would be more perfect if the brain were to be found in the center of the body, like a planets core, in order that all signals coming from the Godform, through the brain, and into the body would in fact be coming from the center. Thus, that body would not be controlled from the top down, but from the center out. This is the manner in which the serpent directs the brain. The brain is considered to be the *higher brain* and it is the seat of highest physical consciousness.

Further, within the same illustration, the reader will see the obvious left/right hemispheres of the brain. These twin hemispheres are commonly considered to be the *left and right brains* and are the areas primarily used by the Light-Body to function within the physical vehicle.

The author here would remind the reader that the instant allusion is concerning the staff's symbolical affiliation with the Light-Body.

The reader should take note that the twin serpents are numbered in pairs from one to five. These five pairs are symbolic of the five lower chakras found in the Light-Body. Here, in the Light-Body, these twin serpents take on the additional allusion to the *solar* and *lunar* nerve energies which intertwine up through the first five chakras to eventually join at the sixth. The *solar* and *lunar* energies travel through three major energy conduits running through the midline of the Light-Body are symbolized by the twin serpents and central staff also. Those energy conduits are referred to as *ida nadi* (left), *pingala nadi* (right) and *sushumna nadi* (middle) in the Hindu doctrines. These conduits meet or join together at the points corresponding to the five lower Spheres and finally at the Third-Eye (wings) where they then end in the nasal breathing mechanism.

The five *points* or pairs of numbers also allude to the respective ruling planet of each of those five chakras as is detailed in the previous section of this chapter. The five chakras alluded to, and thus the twin serpents themselves, are considered to be *time-bound,* so up to the fifth chakra, the practitioner of meditation is still *time-bound.*

Moving upwards along the staff depicted in Illustration 13-B, the reader will find a set of wings connected to the staff itself by a golden strap-device. These wings allude to the sixth chakra called the Ajna Chakra in the Hindu tradition where it is depicted as being a two-petaled Lotus flower; as such, the wings of the staff are a direct correlation to this sixth chakra, the *Third-Eye.* The name Ajna Chakra literally means *command center.*

Likewise, in the Hindu tradition, when a *yogi* performs sound repetition in the sixth chakra, the syllables of his repetition (SOHAM) becomes reversed, forming the mantra HAMS A, which is the Sanskrit word for swan, the bird that can fly to places unknown to ordinary people. So it can be readily seen that again wings at this point in the symbol are the only suitable symbolism for this particular point on the staff.

As noted previously, the solar (masculine) and lunar (feminine) nerve energies join at the point symbolized by the wings. Here, the wings allude to the plane of neutrality and there becomes a balance between the solar and lunar energies within the body. The components of duality become equalized and the wings symbolize the area of the Light-Body that is the divine seat of the half-male, half-female, deity. It is in the chakra symbolized by those wings that the practitioner of the occult arts begins to experience the nectar of immortality (soma) thus gaining the power to remain youthful.

Next, in Illustration 13-B, the reader will notice three golden rings. These rings allude to a three-part chakra, known as the Soma Chakra, which is one of the lesser-chakras contained within the sixth chakra. In the Light-Body these three points are found to reside between the sixth and seventh chakra which would be in the area of the forehead, above the *Third-Eye.*

Finally, the reader comes to the crown or ball residing atop the staff. This golden ball, or golden dome, alludes to the seventh chakra and seat of supreme consciousness within the Light-Body. It is at this place in the Light-Body that the I AM is permanently seated. This seat is the spot at the crown of the head between the two hemispheres of the physical brain of the Material-Body as indicated in Illustration 7-A. Here the practitioner is said to become *realized* and at one with the cosmic principles at play within the body that also govern the entire universe.

As has been shown, it matters not whether the staff of Caduceus is compared to the vehicle known as the Material-Body or the vehicle known as the Light-Body. Each separately, and in unison, are perfectly represented by the staff and thus, no matter which vehicle the Self may be utilizing at any given point, the deity carries the staff.

As described above and as depicted in Illustrations 7-A, 13-B and 13-C, the staff is an accurate description of Our true nature as Illuminati; Our true Self. It perfectly depicts the Dragon, that Winged-Serpent, at the very core of both Our Material -and Light- Bodies. As the reptile resides in each human *He* becomes overwhelmed and suppressed by the strength of the Material-Body and the Ego; *He* only becomes self-aware of *His* true nature when those in whom *He* resides awaken their consciousness, and next the Godform, through the employment of the energy centers symbolized within the Staff of Caduceus.

Just as the Material- and Light-Bodies are reflections of Our true form and just as the staff alludes to those bodies, so must the staff allude to the Illuminati and Reptilian form because those bodies themselves reflect that same form. Thus, the staff itself is seen to allude to the true Illuminati form, the Dragon, the Winged-Serpent.

Just review the Illustrations listed in this chapter. It is easy to meditate, concentrate and see the staff as being the Dragon/Serpent which is at the very core of Our beings.

Illuminati are the Serpent, hibernating within the vehicular *Bodies* patiently awaiting conscious awakening at which point We become the Dragon.

"During meditation, I have literally felt and experienced the shape-shifting of my Light-Body into that of a winged-dragon. During such powerful moments I can feel my form change into that of a dragon and can even later feel the sensations of this change to my Light-Body in different areas of my Material-Body.

At those times when the form of my Light-Body shifts into the form of a Dragon, my entire being is perceived differently. I am able to feel the alterations in my facial-feature, body (where my wings form), thought processes and even the very concept of my identity is new and altered. When my Light-Body is shifted into this form, I know that I AM a serpent being, a winged-serpent, the Dragon.

During those moments, when I am aware of the shape-shifting of my Light-Body, I am reminded of the Dragon Society located in none other than Port Arthur, Japan and am aware of the synchronicity of the fact that I was born in Port Arthur, Texas.

It was not until after I received enlightenment of the meaning of the Staff of Caduceus from the Goddess, Isis, while meditating before Her EYE, that I first experienced turning into the Dragon. After beginning to gain under-

standing that the Staff is none other than an allusion of Our true Self and the reptile form, I began to slowly evolve and my consciousness as the Dragon was made known to me."

The Third-Eye

The term *Third-Eye* is a reference to the Sixth Sphere (chakra) located in the Light-Body in the area corresponding to the area just above the bridge of the nose and between the eyes in the Material-Body. Likewise, the organ of the Material-Body associated with the *Third-Eye* is the pineal gland, a small pinecone shaped gland found in the exact geometrical center of the brain.

In the ancient Hindu texts, the *Third-Eye* is named the *Ajna Chakra* which is translated to mean 'command center'. This title is a fitting title once it is realized that the gland of the Material-Body associated with this chakra, the pineal gland, is considered by medical professionals to be the central gland which controls the functions of the other glands located in the Material-Body.

Before moving along, it should be noted that the pinecone was used symbolically throughout ancient cultures in Indonesia, Babylonia, Sumeria, Egypt, Greece and Rome to represent or portray the highest spiritual illumination. Likewise, it is used in Freemasonry, Theosophy, Gnosticism and Christianity in the same manner. It is no coincidence that the pinecone shaped gland, and the Sixth Sphere, is recognized as the seat of spiritual sight and consciousness. It is not until the dawning or rising of this *inner sun* takes place that spiritual enlightenment, also known as illumination, takes place.

The presence of the pinecone is depicted in numerous paintings, carvings, sculptures and architecture throughout the known world, i.e. Angkor Wat in Cambodia, Statues of Buddha throughout Asia, the Court of the Pinecone in Rome (Vatican), the staff of the Pope, the coat of arms of the Holy See and the wand/staff of Dionysus (Ithyrusus).

When viewing the Masonic Tracing Board known as the *Masters Carpet,* one can clearly see the *All-Seeing Eye,* the *Third-Eye,* with its' radiance shining forth. Likewise, meditation upon the Sixth Sphere causes the Third-Eye to shine brilliantly once the opening of the Sphere has been achieved. Of curious note is that, upon the above-named tracing board just as in the Great Seal of the United States of America, the *Eye* depicted there is none other than the left eye, the Eye of Ra; or, as modern religion likes to refer to Him, the Eye of Lucifer.

The Egyptians believed that the center of the brain (pineal gland) was the Sun or *Eye of God* and the original name for the Eye of Horus was actually the Eye of Ra (the Sun-God).

One of the oldest books in the world known to modern man, the Mayan book called the Bopol Vuhl, pictures the Bright Morning Star, Quetzalcoatal wearing a shining Sun as a crown upon his head in the same manner as the

Egyptian Uraeus Cobra (complete with solar disk) was worn upon the crown of the ruling Pharaoh. The similarities cannot be missed there and it must be considered that the Pharaoh, the MAN, was viewed as the living microcosm to Quetzalcoatl's and the Cobra's macrocosm with but one distinction. The MAN's, Pharaoh, solar disk, or Sun, is inside him and is the *Third-Eye.*

The author here asks the reader to review Illustration 7-A and 13-C. In Illustration 7-A the reader sees the head of the cobra, the serpent that is Our subtlest form of being, residing at the very core or center of the Material-Body. In Illustration 13-C the reader will see the location of the pineal gland (Dot #1) just above the *head* of the serpentine column. Again the meaning of the Mayan and Egyptian allegory cannot be easily missed. The *serpent-god* in those allegories (flying serpent and cobra) is an allusion to the true identity and form of the Godform, the Serpent, lying at the very core of every Material-Body while the crown, depicted in those allegories as the *sun-crown* or disk is none other than the pineal gland. Therefore, if one imagines the reptile, or *serpent-god,* of those allegories as being crowned with the Sun then it must be clear to the enlightened mind that those allegories, in alluding to none other than MAN as the Serpent Godform, is telling Us that Our crown is the opened and active *Third-Eye.*

Illuminati know that We are the Serpent-Gods, crowned with the brilliance of the radiant Sun.

Within the center of the brain, in this Sun, is the key to the union of the inner male and female energies. This center is accordingly also the gateway between the material and ethereal worlds along with the gateway to psychic development.

Sirius is the brightest star in the sky and, being twenty times brighter than Our Sun, is known as the 'Sun behind the Sun', the *Black Sun,* and the true source of Our Sun's potency.

Our Sun being only the sustainer of material life, Sirius is that light keeping the spiritual as well as material realms alive and the True Light in the East associated with none other than the Goddess, Isis. It is associated with the pineal gland and is the Blazing Star of the secret Orders.

The importance and significance of the *Third-Eye* cannot be emphasized enough. It is the awakening or opening of this Sphere that allows for the true attainment of Self-Consciousness which in turn is a necessary prerequisite for the transfer of consciousness from the Material-Body into the Light-Body.

If the pinecone is a fitting metaphor for the state of existence of the pineal gland in the Material-Body then it would be fitting to refer to its' equal in the Light-Body as the purest, clearest, most brilliant diamond reflecting the fire of the *inner-sun.*

Allegorically speaking, where the *macro* consists of the Sun being the material reflection of the Black Suns' spiritual radiance, the *micro* consists of the Material-Body being the reflection of the *Third-Eye's* spiritual radiance.

In both cases, it is but the material acting as the reflection or *effect* of some spiritual radiation of Light, or *cause*.

During meditation, when the Spheres of the Light-Body are opened and the serpent-force ascends to the head (crown chakra/Kether) via the *sushumna nadi*, after neutralizing effects of the *ida* and *pingala nadis*, it is then that the pineal and pituitary glands become stimulated in the Material-Body and important hormonal secretions are activated in those glands. A white, milky type fluid is secreted from the pineal gland while a yellowish, creamy fluid is secreted from the pituitary gland.

When the two secretions are mixed, the meditator experiences a bright flash of light so radiant that the *Third-Eye* opens. This mixed fluid, secreted as described above, is the Holy Water, Elixir of Life, Fountain of Youth, etc. sought by so many historians, philosophers, scientists and occult students. These white and yellow secretions then flow down the pancreatic nerve to the Third Sphere, located in the solar plexus area, where Christ-Consciousness is realized or obtained.

The state of consciousness experienced is so potent that the entire body becomes illuminated and this Light ascends to the crown of the head (Seventh Sphere) where unity with *'GOD'* is experienced or, in other words, where consciousness as the Godform is realized. This is the meaning of Christ's words: "I and the Father are One." (Eye and the Sun are One).

This Light can be seen by the meditator, as well as others looking through their opened *Third-Eye's*, to project outwardly and shine exactly like the Sun, or Light, from his or her illuminated *Third-Eye*.

CHAPTER FOURTEEN

THE FLAMING CHERUB

On several occasions, while in meditation before the Eye, the author was allowed to see a picture or scene behind the Eye where there were two distinct black circles side by side in coexistence. See Illustration 14-A.

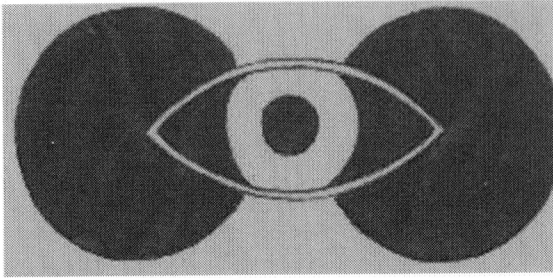

Several times, the author suspected that this occurrence was but the body's re-institution of the dominant use of the physical eyes over the Third-Eye; the physical eyes being what would be termed crossed before coming back into perfect or normal focus. However, this suspicion failed to hold up after numerous sessions of

Illustration 14-A

meditation because, while consciously focusing on the empowerment of the sixth chakra and purposely keeping acute attention on focusing the ethereal light in that particular Sphere of the Light-Body, the vision of the black disks behind the eye continued to occur. Keep in mind that after the Eye became translucent, and the author was able to see the black circles continue to exist behind the Eye, the Eye would return to its normal condition and further meditation would usually ensue.

The author realized that there is a message being sent to him by Her, in this simple vision. The author here asks the reader to re-read the very first sentence of this chapter. Re-read it, please.

Consider that sentence, describing the meditative vision, as a pictoral allegory. Is its meaning not cloaked in riddle? Or, if not riddle, is the meaning of the vision, like visions of prophets, cloaked in unintelligible symbology? On first consideration this seems to be the case exactly and honestly, it is exactly what the author initially supposed after concluding that he was not simply becoming cross-eyed at some point during his focus/concentration meditation on the Eye of Isis.

The author has learned however that his time before the Eye, and time before the image of the Queen of Heaven, Isis, is allowing for the reception of answers to things not previously understood by the author as well as the answer to questions not even asked. Further, pieces of the *puzzle* that previously seemed like random and unique *pictures* have come together to make sense of an elaborate and definitely larger whole.

Below, the author would simply re-write the first sentence of this chapter describing the vision of the circles behind the Eye; however, the author here substitutes the word 'Eye' with the word 'Sun' and the word 'circles ' with the word 'holes':

> *"On several occasions, while in meditation before the Sun, the author was able to see behind the Sun where there were two distinct black holes side by side in coexistence."*

Next, the author would once more substitute the words 'black holes' with the word 'gateways':

> *"On several occasions, while in meditation before the Sun, the author was able to see behind the Sun where there were two distinct gateways side by side in coexistence."*

It is common knowledge that the Sun of the solar-system in which Earth resides is the closest star to Earth as is obvious by the fact that Earth revolves around that star (Sun). The author poses this question: "Is the Sun a star-gate whereby, or through which, humanity can escape Earth-bound existence?" Further, "Is the only way to the *father* through the *son?*"

Contained within the allegories of the Book is the tale of Nimrod and the Tower of Babel. A close scrutiny of that particular tale will inevitably leave the reader with the following impressions:

- The people, under the authority of the mighty hunter (King) Nimrod, were building a tower in order to reach *'GOD'* (the Sun) or heaven;
- The people and tower must have come very close to achieving the goal of ascending to *heaven* and *'GOD'* because in the tale, at some point after their grand ability was noticed by *'GOD'*, He dispersed the people, removing their ability to communicate with one another and subsequently, their ability to accomplish great feats together such as reaching the Sun;
- After that time the people were scattered and the language barrier put an end to any unity that then existed;
- *'GOD'* was angry that Nimrod and his people had almost accomplished their goal of reaching *heaven*.

An understanding of Nimrod's death and ascension to godly status as a Sun-God also lends a peculiar element to an already peculiar story. "Why were the people trying to reach the Sun, *'GOD'*; and what did they intend to do once they would have arrived there?" "Why would *'GOD'* be so infuriated that they had almost achieved their mighty feat?" "Where did the people even get the idea to build a tower tall enough to reach the Sun?"

The author remits the memory of reading a book along the years which briefly outlined the rites and trials that Egyptian initiates were required to pass before it was considered that they had reached *attainment.* The author is at a loss for the title of this book or even the name of the author; however, a Google search of the subject matter may help to reveal these facts.

Anyhow, after reaching *attainment,* those individuals were taken atop the Great Pyramid where they were shown *that which is concealed by the Sun.* The author encourages the reader to study this and find this information for yourselves.

In the writings of Helena Petrovna Blavatsky, Isis Unveiled, Part I, it is written that the Sun is the *'GOD'* of nature and physical or material life. This ancient belief brings to mind another question: "Was the Sun worshipped in ancient times because those people then knew that the Sun concealed the gateway to the heavens?"

Consider Genesis 3:24, where Jehovah places a flaming cherub, with a flaming sword spinning every which way, to guard the entrance to the Garden of Eden in order to prevent humanity from re-entering the Garden and partaking of the Tree of Life.

Is the *Garden* the solar-system, galaxy or universe(s) and is the *cherub,* with the *flaming and spinning sword* who *guards* the entry (gate) into the *Garden* the Sun?

Keep in mind that ALL ancient and superior civilizations were worshippers of the Sun in one way or another. Why? What did the ancient Egyptians know that we do not? Further, where did their empire, and all the people of that empire, go? This same question could be applied to the Atlantean, Mayan, Azteca, Peruvian and other great civilizations whose inhabitants seemed to disappear and vanish from the face of the Earth all at once. Where are the millions-upon-millions of human bones which would be present had those civilizations all *simply* perished in death?

Why is the Sun at the center of every single religion known to man; even Judaism, Christianity and Islam?

Consider next another vision experienced by the author while in meditation before the Eye. During this time, the author saw upon his field of meditation (a black/white checkered board) the unfinished pyramid with the *All-Seeing Eye* above it, though not connected to the pyramid itself. Note here, that the *All-Seeing Eye* described here was the same Eye with which the author is familiar. This pyramid and Eye sat in the center of a *room,* and past the pyramid, at the farthest point from the author's view, was a corner like the corner of a room. The corner itself was a dividing point between two separate hallways; one leading to the left, while the other went right. See Illustration 14-B.

First, let us admit that this vision, at its forefront and center, had a very well-known motif; that is, the unfinished pyramid with the *All-Seeing Eye*

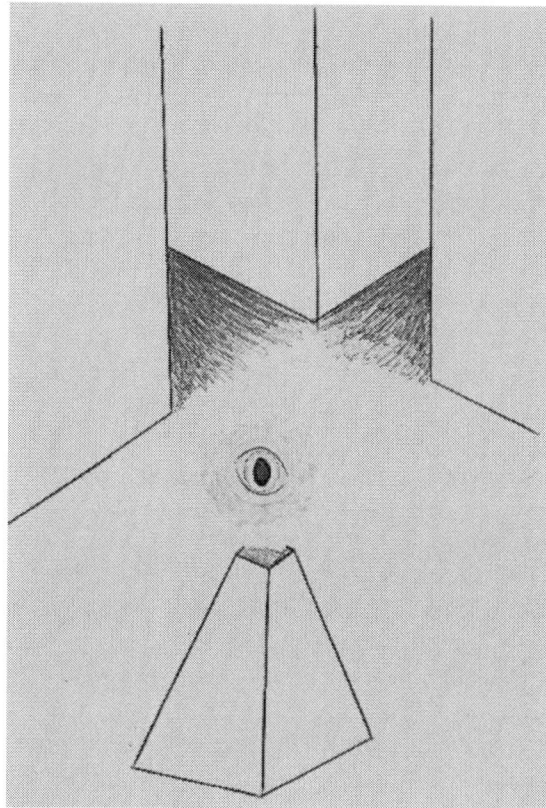

Illustration 14-B

above and separate from it. The fame of this symbol is evidenced by its appearance on the reverse of the seal of the United States of America. Further, who has not had an American dollar in their possession and noticed this same motif thereon?

In the context here, the pyramid with the Eye is not the only point of acute focus. What of the two hallways or paths behind the pyramid/Eye? Where do those hallways lead?

As was done previously, the author would once again substitute the word Eye with the word Sun and the word hallways with the word gateways:

The author saw... the unfinished pyramid with the Sun above it... this pyramid and Sun sat in the center of a room and behind... was a corner which was the... dividing point between two separate gateways; one leading to the left while the other went right.

If the reader would review the illustration on the cover of the instant book, the reader will behold the image of Isis, Queen of Heaven, with twin Ankhs above. Within this image of Isis one can first see the depiction of the Primary Deity, the Black Sun, shining in Her golden radiance. Isis gives life to, and cradles within boundaries, a black disc with red ring as a representation of the Secondary Deity, (Jehovah) who himself emanates the dual aspect Deity of Creation (Sun) depicted therein as the twin Ankhs.

This image of the Winged-Isis is not original; although it is an original rendition of Her as painted by the author after a series of meditations followed by painting. After the image of the Goddess was complete, the author perceived the notion that the illustration board on which he had painted Her image was left with too much blank white space. Due to the fact that Isis is often depicted in Egyptian hieroglyphics carrying the Ankh, the author chose to employ small Ankhs above Her so as to give the illusion that the Ankhs were behind Her at some distance. There, the author placed the two Ankhs in their positions simply for the purpose of symmetry; or so he thought. Those Ankhs were never intended to be a part of the painting from the paintings conception.

After meditating on the image itself, the author was struck with the realization that he had once again manifested the image of the Sun and twin black gateways. This manifestation was not the product of any conscious thought and it was not until much later after the pictures completion that the secondary *theme* of the *gateway* was realized.

Has the reader already realized the synonymy between these distinct meditative visions? In all visions there exist two allegorical gateways whose location is behind the Sun. Now consider the synonymy between these and the unconscious materializations of the same theme in the author's image of Isis as depicted on the cover of the instant manuscript.

In no way does the author submit the idea that he is the only person in possession of this information or who has ever received these visions.

In the vision depicted in Illustration 14-B, there was a pyramid, which presents the question: What was the true purpose of the Great Pyramid? Was it the source of energy needed to ascend to, and enter, the star-gate? If so, how can it be used today for the same purpose?

The current world civilization's time on Earth is ending and it is time that humanity evolves or faces the extinction of this particular Age. Something must be done about it. Is it not agreed that humanity has waited long enough? The time to enlighten mankind (the Masses) is now, in order that They might choose to proceed into evolution alongside Illuminati or be left behind to Their own demise.

It might very well be that the energy that can be raised only by a world of Sun's, a world of *people,* is exactly that which is needed to enter into the *Garden* through the Sun. We MUST challenge the limits of nature as we know them to be. This calls for a global community of Free-Thinkers, no longer bound by the chains of false religions designed to subdue and subjugate mankind.

We MUST insist that the Universal Church in Rome open its' vaults and expose the secret human origin which has been collected and kept hidden for two millennia.

Ancient Illuminati took careful measure to detail the existence of the star-gate in their paintings, poems, stories, statues, etc. Likewise, We must be vigilant and study these works, for they provide the keys lending evidence that this theory was, at that time, a Secret of Secrets.

Why is Jesus referred to as the Son of Man no less than eighty-four times in the New Testament? Is he really the *Sun-Man*? Likewise, why does the Book insist that salvation, through the Son-Man, is the only way to *heaven* and the *Father*? Should it really be stated that the only way to the *Father* is through the *Sun*? The author sets forth that these scriptures, and others like them, are not merely coincidences but are pieces of a larger code that must be deciphered.

Consider the lyrics of a popular Hip-Hop song from the 1990's by the famous rapper known as Nas: "... and we'll walk right into the Sun, we won't land; We'll walk right into the Sun, Hand in hand; If I ruled the world, I'd free all my Sons; I love 'em, love 'em baby, black diamonds and pearls; If I ruled the world..."

Humanity needs men and women no longer bound by what has been taught to them. Mankind needs free-thinkers, living gods, who possess complete liberation of mind. Freedom of this kind can only be gained when the doctrines of religion are set aside and the true teachings of the Holy Books are put into practice in the manner in which the prophets meant for their teachings to be practiced; however, such can only take place when one receives the Illumination of the Goddess.

Are you one of Us?

CHAPTER FIFTEEN

THE LAW OF EIGHT AND

REALITY OF FOUR

"Do not hesitate to use [the LAW] for any purpose which is constructive.
It is no more selfish to use spiritual law for personal purposes than it is to plant a garden for your own personal use."

-Ernest Holmes
This Thing Called You
p. 41

DO AS YE WILL; HARM NOT A ONE.

Above, written in bold capital letters, is the *law of eight* as set forth through the Wiccan Path. It is referred to as the *law of eight* because it sets forth in eight words THE LAW as taught to those who aspire to that particular Path of the Luciferian Doctrine(s). The *law of eight* is very much a two-part 'face-value' statement meant to afford the practicing magician with:

(1) Knowledge of THE LAW that governs Our existence in the Material-Body; and,

(2) Knowledge of the responsibility that ensues from the use of that LAW, no matter whether it is used knowingly or ignorantly.

DO AS YE WILL is a reference to the free-will that exists within the limits of human manipulation of material reality, including the spiritual energies, and also the beings governing that material reality. It is the free-will that is the envy of even the highest of the spiritual beings for, whilst some of those beings are destined to be forever what they are, humans, or better yet, the Godform within humans, have the ability to become *'GOD'* because of the existence of free-will.

Outside of certain laws of Nature, free-will allows the individual to do or cause anything to happen, even creation and death, he or she chooses to do or cause. This ability obviously grows in those who are magically or spiritually adept; at that time, the individual has realized his or her free-will to step outside, or away from, the very laws of Nature, Time and Finite-Reality. This is a trait of the Godform and as such, the mechanism, or bio-computer We call

140

the Material-Body, which is the vehicle of the Godform, is the only creature of the Earth endowed with this ability. For *MAN* has *become like* the Gods, remember?

Even the word ability is not a proper explanation. For, free-will is actually the ONLY LAW that the Godform, and thus *MAN,* is bound to. For this reason the individual is bound by no other LAW than the free-will choice he or she makes under the only LAW existing for him or her. Any boundary upon his or her free-will is a boundary instituted solely by him or her despite any outside influence or persuasion.

As such, before the Law of Eight and Reality of Four can be understood, it must be known and accepted that the whole of the LAW is: DO WHAT THOU WILL.

Anything other than those four words places restraint on the very concept (free-will) which is the inherited position of the Godform in relation to all other aspects of the created universe. Only Illuminati ever realize the Truth of THE LAW; the Truth that there is no other LAW.

Next, the second portion of the *law of eight* must be considered. The reader may have realized that the last four words in the *law of eight* seem to be in conflict with the first four words; and they are! The last four words, HARM NOT A ONE, consist of a boundary or limitation placed on the first four. That is the reason that the author has named *this* chapter of the instant book *The Law of Eight and Reality of Four.* This *reality of four* refers to the reality of the last four words contained in the *law of eight.*

Firstly and most simply put, HARM NOT A ONE is a choice encompassed within the real and true LAW. To do what one wills, all-the-while causing no harm or interference in the life or free-will of others, is a choice made by the individual Godform of how, or how not, to exercise THE LAW. They represent a choice in the manner in which one chooses to *practice* THE LAW and these last four words can easily be put into practice by anyone following any Path or practicing any Craft.

The *reality of four* secondly represents the responsibility that one acquires after becoming aware of the higher principles of the universe represented in supreme mathematics or sacred geometry and next a full and complete understanding of the whole of THE LAW. When the individual becomes aware, truly aware, he or she is considered enlightened, or Illuminati. If that individual were NOT Illuminati, enlightenment would not dawn for him or her in the first place, for that dawning happens only through spiritual influences radiating from the very core of existence: the Primary Deity, the Black Sun.

Enlightenment brings responsibility and it truly should be viewed that the practice of THE LAW is best exercised when one *chooses* to place the exercise of free-will within the boundaries of "harming or interfering with no other persons free-will"; however, enlightenment and the Tree of Life also bring the knowledge that We are not bound by Our responsibility and may choose to harm anyone, or interfere with their free-will, if and when it be Our WILL. True, there might be consequences set into motion by Our WILL; however, that is beside the point. This is the *'Reality of the Four'*: it is ONLY a *choice* of how to individually exercise THE LAW.

Thirdly, the last four words of the *law of eight* warn and remind the practitioner of free-will, and the magician also, of one law which cannot be avoided or circumvented. That law is the *Law of Three* which states: "BIDE THE LAW OF THREE; WHAT YE PUT OUT COMES BACK TO THEE."

This is that which some people call *KARMA*. Jesus is quoted as teaching: "That which Ye sow, so shall Ye reap." In the *'law of three'* *Karmic debt* is referenced and a three-fold multiplication of the *harm* or intrusion upon the free-will is repaid to the one causing *harm*.

Although *karma* is a law that cannot be evaded, even by the Godform, THE LAW still supersedes, for if an individual who has caused *harm* is enlightened, he or she might take measures to pay this *Karmic debt* while still in existence in his or her Material-Body. Through exercising free-will one may choose to right a wrong and thereby one may clear their *Karmic debt*. Further along this same line of thought, it is taught that through meditation upon the Sixth Sphere, the *Third-Eye,* the release of *Karmic debt* is realized. In this light then, it truly is in the best interest of the enlightened individual to practice THE LAW in its extended version as set forth by Wicca and by the author presently, as the Reality of Four.

Understanding the Law of Eight and Reality of Four is a prerequisite to rising above the Tree of Knowledge of Good and Evil and partaking of the Tree of Life. For, although Wicca does teach the normally *best* concept of the application of THE LAW, Aleister Crowely set it forth all-the-more correctly and clearly. When it comes to the manipulation and use of universal ethers, DO WHAT THOU WILL is the whole law and THE LAW is complete within those four words.

Likewise, the guiding principles of the universe continuously seek the path of least resistance. Electricity, water and air all do the same; furthermore, an eagle will use the currents of the air as a tool to glide upon in order to travel to-and-fro rather than exerting the energy required to fly against the wind.

Even when one views the paths of the planets around the Sun, one sees evidence of the path of least resistance. The Earth does not struggle against the pull of the Sun's gravitational force; rather, the Earth submits to this pull and planetary rotation ensues. The sum of that particular equation is clearly evident; through *that* path of least resistance, LIFE occurs on the one in submission: Earth. So it must be also with Us. To experience true life, not the life of materiality, but the true and spiritual life, We must submit to the path of least resistance and choose the creation of a self-imposed boundary of free-will. That is, the exercise of free-will to choose to limit that free-will for the betterment of the whole. That boundary, made by the compass, can never be permanent and each individual chooses whether or how to exercise free-will as he or she chooses.

Put simply, this means DO NOT do to others what you know they would be inclined to do unto you; rather, it means do unto others as you would want them to do unto you. That, of course, is the Golden Rule; yet still, one retains the *choice* of how to exercise his or her WILL.

This path of least resistance is an underlying current in the nature of the created universe and is the key to spiritual enlightenment and the evolution of the Light-Body after becoming conscious of the Godform. Once these take place along the path of least resistance, it is found that the cause(s) and effect(s) of everyday life are not happening to, or effecting, the Godform, the 'I'. Along the path of least resistance the 'I', who is *'GOD'*, becomes simply a viewer of all cause and effect taking place. Before that time, it would have seemed that both cause and effect were happening to, and thus effecting, the 'I'. For those reasons, uniting the WILL with the path of least resistance begins to cause less *experience* of the day to day material life and less *experience* means less *association* as the Ego. It is precisely this *association* as the Ego, along with *experience,* which leads to *Karmic debt.* Less *association* as the Ego will lead to unity *with* and *as* GOD and the 'I' will begin to cease to incur that *Karmic debt* little by little and even begin to erase that *debt* after time.

It is for this reason that the author promotes the path of least resistance, as taught by The Craft in the *Law of Eight,* as the optimal way to enlightenment; however, even the author still retains his inherited right to practice THE LAW in whatever manner he so chooses. The way in which the author chooses to practice that LAW is the way which causes no harm to others. This practice comes second only to the knowledge, wisdom and understanding of THE LAW. This second-place status is only due to the fact that the Truth of THE LAW will allow for the perfect practice of THE LAW. Until that is obtained, the Godform only experiences 'Self' through the Ego and *Karmic debt* cannot be relinquished.

Truth shall set you free. It can erase a destiny of further or repeated imprisonments within the *muddy vesture of decay.*

Through Truth one learns that he or she, like *'GOD',* has the power to choose to do anything one desires; however, when one chooses not to, that one becomes the *Sun.*

CHAPTER SIXTEEN

FAITH WITHOUT WORK IS MOOT

Here and now the author provides an exercise to be practiced steadfastly, that is, routinely, in order to bring forth personal evidence of the ability to build the Light-Body.

As the occult student most likely already knows, the 'Self' possesses four separate bodies which help to conceal the I AM. Those bodies are commonly known as Desire-, Thought-, Ether -and Dense- Bodies. These bodies may also be referred to by other names or forms, depending on the particular school of thought one may adhere to. For example, the Ether-and Dense-Bodies are also referred to as the Astral- and Physical; Subtle- and Food- as well as Light- and Material, respectively.

Here, the Ether/Astral-Body will be referred to as the Light-Body and the Dense/Physical-Body will be referred to as the Material-Body in the keeping with the theme of the instant manuscript. The author will not reference either the Thought-Body or the Desire-Body, for not much work can be accomplished in these bodies without first the accomplishment of at least some work in the Light -and Material- Bodies. Mostly, it is the evolution of the latter two bodies which directly provide a link to change in the Desire- and Thought-Bodies.

The Light-Body, which will be the main subject during this exercise, is referred to as Spirit in orthodox religious doctrines such as Judaism, Christianity and Islam. Although they only perceive the existence and importance of the Light-Body in a warped and convoluted sense, these doctrines are correct in their assertion that the Light-Body *(spirit)* is closer to who and what We really are than is the Material-Body. In ancient Egypt, the Light-Body was referred to as the *ka;* in Tai-Chi it is the *chi*; in Taoism it is the *ki;* and in the Kabbalah, it is one of the *kli's.*

As covered previously in this book, within the Light-Body there exist seven centers commonly known as chakras and here referred to as Spheres. These Spheres are centers of cosmic energies which exist in each and every Light-Body on the planet. Many people live out their entire lives never becoming conscious of the existence of these energy centers, much less ever learning how to activate and use them.

Additionally, the Spheres relate to and are a microcosm of, the seven major planets; further, it is the energies and magnetism of those planets which accumulate into the Spheres of Our Light-Bodies. As a group, the Sphere's existence within Our Light-Body represents the solar-system in which we are not only a part of but actually are. We are the microcosm and direct reflection of the solar-system (macrocosm).

144

The I AM is allowed free-will and conscious control over these Spheres and the building of the Temple of Solomon includes the opening, exercise, strengthening and use of the Light-Body through the development of the Spheres.

As explained previously the Spheres do not actually exist in the Material-Body although the energy may be felt in the areas of the Material-Body where the Spheres' existence in the Light-Body coincides with that of the Material-Body. For a brief overview of each chakra and its' correlation to both the Light -and Material- Bodies please refer back to Chapter Thirteen.

Exercise

The instant exercise is meant to be practiced by couples, or in pairs, although formal marriage is not required.

Access to the primeval force lay in the 'Helper' (Eve, the woman) and this force can be tapped into by the joining of this primeval force with the creative force found in the male.

Through the sexual-union of this exercise, access to the Light of the Black Sun, will be realized by utilizing the material incarnation of the *Goddess*: the female; woman. Woman is the conduit whereby Man can tap into the primeval forces in order to create.

The above statement does not imply some gross physical intercourse or crude act of sexual intercourse; but rather, a technique wherein the physical union of the Material-Bodies become a conduit or pathway for the ethereal energy of the *Goddess* to flow from the ethereal realm, into the incarnated *God*, and back to its original source: the *Goddess*.

When the joining of the Sun (man) and Earth (woman) take place, the very powers of both the primeval universe and the created universe are present and can be channeled into the Light-Body for the purpose of illuminating the seven Spheres. Deep meditation and the opening of the chakras can be realized when this union of the incarnate *God* and *Goddess* takes place.

The author warns that this exercise should only be practiced with great care and respect for the forces that will eventually be under the practitioners' control, for these forces are the very forces of LIFE and DEATH.

- In a seated position, with his back against a wall, chair-back, sofa-back, etc., the nude male should sit with his heels on the floor (or seat of chair/sofa) and knees slightly spread.
- The nude female should sit either facing away from or towards the male (i.e., her back or front torso should be resting against the male's chest/abdomen) taking careful measure to impale her body upon the male's penis without over stimulating him.

The male's penis should remain deeply impaled into the female's vagina. No in-and-out motion should take place as this practice, though sexual in nature, is not being performed for the purpose of physical intercourse, sexual stimulation of the genatalia or other gratification of the Light-Body and Material-Body.

- In this position the man and woman should take the time necessary to completely relax and join together in unity of mind, body and essence (soul). No time limit can be placed on this step and the pair should become as comfortable in their positions as is possible. The author recommends that the couple spend at least ten to twenty minutes simply relaxing and becoming aware of one another's body and energies.

Different ways to relax might include talking, sparingly sharing food/drink such as fresh fruit, juice or water (alcohol should be strictly avoided), body massage (no over-stimulation of the vagina or penis which might cause orgasm or ejaculation), oil rubs, listening to music etc. Other ways to relax might include the use of candle-light, music designed specifically for use as a meditation or astral-travel aid, incense, pictorial aides such as images of the God/Goddess of one's choice (no pornography), designs and symbols meant to ease one into certain moods or representations of the five elements, etc.

Note that the intended purpose here is to completely relax into one another in order that your two separate identities become one *higher* body which can be compared to the singular aspect of divinity in possession of both the masculine and feminine energies and qualities; or, in other words, to manifest in the original form, the Elohim, the very creators of creation.

DO NOT CAUSE ONE ANOTHER TO REACH ORGASM OR OTHERWISE EJACULATE. To do so is to either end the exercise (for those persons whose Light-Body is not strong) or greatly diminish the desired effects of this holy meditative practice.

- After relaxation and unity is achieved, the couple should begin to focus on opening and tapping into the First Sphere. This process should be focused on together, jointly, as if the couple were a single mind and being.

Take time to ensure that this Sphere is open in both persons before attempting to move on. Take the time necessary for both partners to not only feel the effects of the energy within their Light-Body, but also the time necessary for both partners to become familiar and at ease with the sensations they are feeling. This process should not be rushed, as rushing could lead to over-stimulation of the Material-Body and an accidental release (orgasm/ejaculation) of the energies being utilized during this technique. It is of utmost importance that both partners are comfortable with the practice.

Quiet, simple and minimal communication is allowed, if needed, until realization of the empowerment of the chakras can be achieved without it. *Do not be afraid to communicate with your partner.*

- Once the First Sphere is opened and its presence is felt in the Light-Body, the couple should silently meditate, taking measure to remain still and allow the Material-Body to *slow down* while becoming one with the other. All thought should be suspended for as long as is possible and breathing should be slowed and timed so as to be in unison one with the other. Spend ten to twenty minutes if possible meditating on and experiencing the energy of this Sphere while in the state of the *higher and unified being.*

If any thoughts appear in the mind, simply set them aside and refocus on the energy and on breathing in unison with your partner.

- After spending the necessary time basking in the light of the First Sphere, the couple should begin to focus on opening and tapping into the Second Sphere.

Again, this process should be focused on together, jointly, as if the couple were of a single mind and being.

Again, take the required time to ensure that this Sphere is open in both persons before attempting to move on. Take the time necessary for both partners to not only feel the effects of the energy within their Light-Body, but also the time necessary for both partners to become familiar and at ease with the sensations they are feeling. Similar to the opening of the previous Sphere, this process should not be rushed, as rushing could lead to over-stimulation of the Material-Body.

Quiet, simple and minimal communication is allowed if needed until realization of the empowerment of the chakras can be achieved without it. *Do not be afraid to communicate with your partner.*

- Once the Second Sphere is opened and its presence is felt in the Light-Body, the couple should silently meditate, taking measure to remain still and allow the Material-Body to *slow down* while becoming one with the other . All thought should be suspended for as long as is possible and breathing should be slowed and timed so as to be in unison one with the other. Spend ten to twenty minutes if possible meditating on and experiencing the energy of this Sphere while in the state of the *higher and unified being.*

If any thoughts appear in the mind, simply set them aside and refocus on the energy and on breathing in unison with your partner.

- After spending the necessary time basking in the light of the Second Sphere, the couple should begin to focus on opening and tapping into the Third Sphere. Again, this process should be focused on together, jointly, as if the couple were of a single mind and being.

Just as in the previous two steps, take the required time to ensure that this Sphere is open in both persons before attempting to move on. Take the time necessary for both partners to feel the effects of the energy within their Light-Body, as well as the time necessary to become familiar and at ease with the sensations they are feeling. Similar to the opening of the previous Sphere, this process should not be rushed, as rushing could lead to over-stimulation of the Material-Body.

Quiet, simple and minimal communication is allowed until realization of the empowerment of the Sphere can be achieved without it. *Do not be afraid to communicate with your partner.*

- Once the Third Sphere is opened and its presence is felt in the Light-Body, the couple should silently meditate, taking measure to remain still and allow the Material-Body to *slow down* while remaining one with the other . All thought should be suspended for as long as is possible and breathing should be slowed and timed so as to be in unison one with the other. Spend ten to twenty minutes if possible meditating on and experiencing the energy of this Sphere while in the state of the *higher and unified being.*

If any thoughts appear in the mind, simply set them aside and refocus on the energy and breathing in unison with your partner.

- After spending the necessary time basking in the light of the Third Sphere, the couple should begin to focus on opening and tapping into the Fourth Sphere. Again, this process should be focused on together, jointly, as if the couple were of a single mind and being.

Just as in the previous three steps, take the required time to ensure that this Sphere is open in both persons before attempting to move on. Take the time necessary for both partners to feel the effects of the energy within their Light-Body. Similar to the opening of the previous Sphere, this process should not be rushed, as rushing could lead to over-stimulation of the Material-Body.

Quiet, simple and minimal communication is still allowed until realization of the empowerment of the Sphere can be achieved without it. *Do not be afraid to communicate with your partner.*

- Once the Fourth Sphere is opened and its presence is felt in the Light-Body, the couple should silently meditate, taking measure to remain still and allow the Material-Body to *slow down* while remaining one with the other. All thought should be suspended for as long as is possible and breathing should be slowed and timed so as to be in unison one with the other. Spend ten to twenty minutes if possible meditating on and experiencing the energy of this Sphere while in the state of the *higher and unified being.*

If any thoughts appear in the mind, simply set them aside and refocus on the energy and breathing in unison with your partner.

- After spending the necessary time basking in the light of the Fourth Sphere, the couple should begin to focus on opening and tapping into the Fifth Sphere. Again, this process should be focused on together, jointly, as if the couple were of a single mind and being.

Just as in the previous four steps, take the required time to ensure that this Sphere is open in both persons before attempting to move on. Take the time necessary for both partners to feel the effects of the energy within their Light-Body. Similar to the opening of the previous Sphere, this process should not be rushed, as rushing could lead to over-stimulation of the Material-Body.

Quiet, simple and minimal communication is still allowed until realization of the empowerment of the Sphere can be achieved without it. *Do not be afraid to communicate with your partner.*

- Once the Fifth Sphere is opened and its presence is felt in the Light-Body, the couple should silently meditate, taking measure to remain still and allow the Material-Body to *slow down* while remaining one with the other. All thought should be suspended for as long as is possible and breathing should be slowed and timed so as to be in unison one with the other. Spend ten to twenty minutes if possible meditating on and experiencing the energy of this Sphere while in the state of the *higher and unified being.*

If any thoughts appear in the mind, simply set them aside and refocus on the energy and breathing in unison with your partner.

- After spending the necessary time basking in the light of the Fifth Sphere, the couple should begin to focus on opening and tapping into the Sixth Sphere. Again, this process should be focused on together, jointly, as if the couple were of a single mind and being.

Just as in the previous five steps, take the required time to ensure that this Sphere is open in both persons before attempting to move on. Take the time necessary for both partners to feel the effects of the energy within their Light-Body. Similar to the opening of the previous Sphere, this process should not be rushed, as rushing could lead to over-stimulation of the Material-Body.

Quiet, simple and minimal communication is still allowed until realization of the empowerment of the Sphere can be achieved without it. *Do not be afraid to communicate with your partner.*

- Once the Sixth Sphere is opened and its presence is felt in the Light-Body, the couple should silently meditate, taking measure to remain still and allow the Material-Body to *slow down* while remaining one with the other . All thought should be suspended for as long as is possible and breathing should be slowed and timed so as to be in unison one with the other. Spend ten to twenty minutes if possible meditating on and experiencing the energy of this Sphere while in the state of the *higher and unified being.*

If any thoughts appear in the mind, simply set them aside and refocus on the energy and breathing in unison with one's partner.

- After spending the necessary time basking in the light of the Sixth Sphere, the couple should begin to focus on opening and tapping into the Seventh Sphere. Again, this process should be focused on together, jointly, as if the couple were of a single mind and being.

Just as in the previous six steps, take the required time to ensure that this Sphere is open in both persons before attempting to move on and take the time necessary for both partners to feel the effects of the energy within their Light-Body. Similar to the opening of the previous Sphere, this process should not be rushed, as rushing could lead to over-stimulation of the Material-Body.

Quiet, simple and minimal communication is still allowed until realization of the empowerment of the Sphere can be achieved without it. *Do not be afraid to communicate with your partner.*

- Once the Seventh Sphere is opened and its presence is felt in the Light-Body, the couple should silently meditate, taking measure to remain still and allow the Material-Body to *slow down* while remaining one with the other . All thought should be suspended for as long as is possible and breathing should be slowed and timed so as to be in unison one with the other. Spend ten to twenty minutes if possible meditating on and experiencing the energy of this Sphere while in the state of the *higher and unified being.*

If any thoughts appear in the mind, simply set them aside and refocus on the energy and breathing in unison with one's partner.

- After spending the necessary time basking in the light of the Seventh Sphere, the couple should begin to focus on the energies of all seven Spheres while simultaneously paying attention to the *Kundalini* rising up the spinal column and thru the Spheres. Again, this process should be focused on together, jointly, as if the couple were of a single mind and being.

Quiet, simple and minimal communication is still allowed until realization of the empowerment of the Sphere can be achieved without it. *Do not be afraid to communicate with your partner.*

Note here that if the participants spent ten to twenty minutes meditating on each Sphere along the way, approximately seventy to one hundred-forty minutes will have passed. If more time is needed, or even desired, it should be taken since there is no time limit or duration required as a *per se* rule for this exercise.

The next step here requires one of the partners to act as a meditative guide for the couple. Either can guide the meditation; however, if one of the two are more advanced in the meditation upon the chakras, the author suggest that he or she be the guide because this guidance will require speech at its' on-set.

- With all seven Spheres opened in both persons, the *guide* should begin to describe the following flow of energy for the other partner[2] so as to create a mental picture and atmosphere whereby both may experience the transfer and flow of energy being described:

  - Picture and feel the Ether, the Light, the primeval force of the Primary Deity entering through the Seventh Sphere (located at the crown of the head) of the female partner impaled upon the male's sexual organ. Now feel the Light of the Goddess enter into the female's Light-Body, flowing down into the Sixth Sphere. Feel the warmth and pulsing sensations as Her Light begins to slowly permeate the female's entire being. Feel the Light flow down into the Fifth, Fourth, Third, Second and First Spheres. Now let the female become aware of pushing this energy out of her First Sphere, through the vagina's equivalent in the Light-Body and into the penis's equivalent in the male's Light-Body.

  - The male should now be guided (unless he is guiding) to experience the flow of the Goddess's energy up through his Spheres from First to Seventh. Next the energy should be sent up and out of the male's Light-Body back to the ethereal Light.

  - Experience and bask in the flow of energy which is being drawn from the universe through the female, passed along to and shared with the male, and released back into the universe. Take time to look into one another's eyes and know that together, as ONE, you are a direct conduit of the same FORCE (WILL of the GODDESS) that flows through the Sun, Moon, Earth, planets, stars, galaxies and entire universe.

  - Enjoy as much time as is desired in this state of union between the Goddess and God.

Remember that the 'female' is the conduit of the universal force. While performing the previous steps in this exercise both participants should mentally picture their entire Light-Bodies slowly combining so as to create one Light-Being. This new Body, which is born of the unity of the Goddess and

---

[2] The exact words given here need not be spoken verbatim. As long as the guides' words relate the same information and guidance, all is well.

God, should be seen growing brighter and brighter the longer the two remain as one. The brighter this Body becomes the stronger it should feel. Though this Body will become stronger and stronger, and will seem to become brighter and more real the longer you allow the energy to loop through you, in no way should the Body, and later the individual Light-Bodies, be viewed as a corporeal or material object. Yes, you will eventually begin to see these bodies easily once the *Third-Eye* is awakened; however, they are made of Light and are a much more subtle form of matter than the gross material form in which the essence of the 'I' currently resides.

If the couple so desires, it is during the flow of this energy while the Spheres are still open that sex-magic may be performed because the presence of the energies in the five lower Spheres effectively ensures the presence of all five elements. If a magical or other form of ritual is not performed at this point, it may be performed at a later point, as detailed below, after the Spheres are closed and after evoking the Elements in a more widely recognized fashion:

- At this point any amount of time can be taken to meditate and still the mind while the ethereal Light loops through the created singularity. During this stage of the exercise, the participants should not focus and concentrate on the chakra energies themselves but should practice meditation and stillness of the mind in order to allow all aspects of creation to dissolve into Supreme Consciousness. There is no time-limit for this step.
- When satisfied, reverse the flow of energy from universe to male, male to female and female back to universe.

When the participants so choose, and when they are ready to end this meditative practice, time should be taken to close each Sphere, in reverse order, taking one to two minutes to close each Sphere. If more time is needed to close each Sphere, this time should be taken. Once all Spheres have been closed, the couple should spend a few minutes discussing the experience and communicating any thoughts, feelings or impressions that came about during any point in the above-listed exercise.

Still being connected to one another physically, care should still be taken not to over stimulate the Material-Body so as to prevent orgasm or ejaculation and effort must be taken to avoid the same.

If a repetition of the meditative cycle is desired, a short break can be taken to relieve the body, enjoy refreshment or any other reason; however, if repeating the meditative cycle is desired, the participants should remain vigilant to maintain a contemplative and spiritual state of consciousness during any break. If no repetition of the meditative cycle will be pursued, the couple can then decide whether or not to physically complete the experience of sexual union by reaching orgasm.

If the male is of a powerful makeup, esoterically speaking, he might here choose to stimulate the female to the point of orgasm and ejaculation, using only his hands and taking care not to become over stimulated himself lest he release the holy-power. He may bring the female to orgasm one or more times as is desired or necessary. This process can be performed with the male genatalia still inside the female sexual organ or without being connected in this manner.

Even if the male plans to reach the point of orgasm himself, time should be taken to allow the release of energy from the female first (by herself) unless the pair plan to use the harnessed energies during a sex-magic ritual which can be performed at this point.

If the sex act is desired unto completion by the couple, any manner of sexual performance may be performed; however, it is the author's opinion that the experience should remain contemplative, pseudo-spiritual and intensely intimate in keeping with the theme of unity of the God/Goddess.

If the couple is versed in magic they may evoke the blessing of the Elements and perform their ritual(s) according to whichever Path of Light they personally adhere to. As is normally the case, the author opines that after the proper rite is performed, the Great Rite should be undertaken so as to cause both male and female to orgasm and ejaculate SIMULTANEOUSLY, being certain that the female and then male speak their WILL into existence during the on-set of orgasm. Any other form of ritual or practice with which the participants are familiar with may be performed during this sex-rite.

Next perform any ritual required by that particular Path and follow by closing the *circle;* being sure to thank the Elements for their presence and blessing.

This meditative exercise will help the couple to build their Light-Bodies and empower one another with cosmic energy from the Primary Deity which is the source of all existence. This practice may be performed any number of times and at any time of the day or night; however, if specific magical intent is desired, attention to the ruling planets, days of the week, hours of the day, colors, stones, etc. should be noted just as when undertaking other magical exercises intended to bring about the fruition of will and desire. Charts outlining this information can easily be obtained through literature on the subject such as, but not limited to, *The Lesser Key of Solomon* as interpreted by A. Crowely.

It must be understood that, unlike the female whose source of cosmic energy is un-ending and cannot be depleted due to her direct union with the Light, the males' ability to harness and utilize that force is limited and becomes less and less potent with each orgasm because each orgasm steals this force from him and returns it unto the female and source from which it was received. Whereas the female acts as a capacitor, re-charging with energy as soon as it has been depleted or released from her body, the male must be charged by the Sun and must hold onto the energy he receives. At times, the energy will escape from the male of its own volition such as in those instances commonly referred to as 'wet-dreams' where the male will ejaculate while in a dreaming state and inadvertently release the holy-elixir. The female is at an advantage because, esoterically speaking, she *is* the source of the males potency.

This exercise is a potent undertaking and should not be used for profane sexual inclinations. This form of yoga should only be performed by those who possess serious and solemn respect for one another and the forces they seek to unify with. Those forces are the primal-forces of the universe. It is no game. With knowledge, understanding and wisdom comes responsibility. With power and ability comes the same and cursed are they who, after attainment, do not remain upright.

You may realize that your consciousness (your partners also) has reached a new level of intensity and reality and may also find that the bond between you and your partner has also begun to grow and intensify.

Visualization

After the above-described exercise, where each Sphere was being energized and awakened in the Light-Bodies of the male and female, conscious notation should be made to ascertain any and all feelings, energies, vibrations, thoughts, knowledge or other super-sensory input which might have accompanied the awakening of each individual Sphere. The same should be noted concerning the period when all Spheres were open at once and during the meditative period where all thought and self-consciousness subsided.

As each of the Spheres are energized and awakened in the Light-Bodies of the male and female, both partners should picture their Light-Bodies as being the same basic form as that of their Material-Bodies but being made up of a bright or luminous whitish/bluish/greenish light energy rather than skin and hair. Both should mentally picture each Sphere bursting into life and glowing red, orange, yellow, green, blue, indigo and violet according to the proper Sphere/Color relationship explained earlier. The participants should see these energy orbs existing within their Light-Body, immersed within the luminous hue that the Light-Body is made up of.

Preparation

Some couples might take more or less time to prepare for the preceding exercise beforehand, setting up tools or instruments which they will use to guide them during this type of meditation. The following is a list of tools which might commonly be employed during this technique; however, the use of aids or tools is not limited to those listed here and every practitioner of meditation and/or magic should be aware that one should use aids with which one is most familiar and most comfortable with.

- Poster-board with seven circles, drawn vertically one above the other, and colored to correspond with the color of the Sphere represented by each respective circle. Always be sure to situate the board so that the First Sphere (Red) is located at the bottom. Also be aware of the place in the room where you intend to place the board and whether or not you and your partner will be facing the same direction or facing each other so as to be looking in two different directions. In that case, two boards might be used; one placed where you can easily view the board without bodily movement or eye strain and the other placed where your partner can view the board in the same relaxed manner.

- Candles should be used rather than electric light. This is so that the illumination of the room is that of a soft glow rather than hard shine. Further, Red, Blue, Yellow, White and Green candles may be used a representation of the *five witnesses,* the Elements. Likewise, seven candles corresponding to the color of each Sphere can be utilized in lieu of the above-noted poster-board. Again, these aids should be able to be viewed by both partners or a duplicate set can be employed.

- If a fireplace is available, this can be used for lighting rather than candles if desired.

- Incense of one's own choice can be lit so as to diffuse any negative energies present within the atmosphere as well as to place the participants in the preferred state of consciousness. Many incense distributors and retailers will have a list of incense odors along with a description of what state of consciousness or skill (such as astral meditation) that particular incense is known to evoke from the mind. Some incense may be mixed while others may not be. Pay close attention to the ingredients or *blends* of incense.

- Incense Oils may be purchased and used for multiple purposes. First, an oil diffuser may be obtained and the oil used in lieu of the more commonly utilized incense that must be burned; or, scented oil may be used along with the burn-type incense. Secondly, these scented oils may be massaged into the skin of either partner. These oils may be added to non-scented oil, such as baby oil, and used to relax and/or stimulate either partner such as through massage or use in the lubrication of the skin.

- Music is a good meditation aid and many albums can be purchased which explicitly focus on the use of notes and instruments to slow the minds cycles-per-minute and guide the meditator into the Alpha State for deep meditation. Other themes are nature, classical music and opera albums. Mostly, one should seek easily flowing rhythms that have a fair amount of low-end frequencies more commonly known as bass. Wendy Rule is a talented occult composer and the first musician that comes to the mind of the author when considering the subject.

- An image of one's preferred Goddess, God or other Deity may be employed as a focal point during this meditation if the couple plans to employ this form of meditation as a prerequisite to sex-magic. Again, both partners should be able to view the image(s) and, at least for the duration of this exercise, should be in agreement of which Deity will be focused on. This image can be a statue, carving, painting, drawing or other type of picture.
- Book of Occult/Esoteric knowledge to read from and discuss during the relaxation periods or breaks. This type of aid can help to maintain a spiritual atmosphere and state of mind if the energies present become over-sexual or during times when the body might need to be relieved.

Loss of the Vital Energy

Though it is not required or expected that all who practice yoga or meditation live a purely celibate life, it is recommended that all possess a complete understanding of the basic knowledge of the practice and purpose of preserving the vital energy.

Almost one hundred percent of the goal of spirituality is attained when one achieves control over all sensual experiences. The most powerful impulse and instinct of the Material-Body, after breathing, is procreation. Therefore, of all that one must master before achieving the ultimate goal, control of his or her sexuality is the most difficult and important.

The universal and cosmic energy, which forms and perpetuates the galaxies and worlds, is the very same energy which is found to be infinitely vibrating within the body and mind of humanity. This life-energy, the *Light of the Black Sun,* manifests on the gross physical level as the semen found in the Material-Body; the same energy manifests on the spiritual level as the sexual energy sustaining and empowering the Light-Body. When this energy is controlled and then sublimated, it is transformed into Spiritual Light. The sexual energy will naturally move in a downward direction toward the lower Spheres and plexuses of the Light- and Material-Bodies associated with sexuality. When controlled and sublimated, the Spiritual Light moves upward, away from those sexual centers and is stored in the higher Spheres and centers of the brain. The Spiritual Light is the creative power, the vital energy, the vigor in a person who has converted sensuality into spirituality.

As noted previously, during the sexual experience, the vital energy is released and lost. Through celibacy, and control of the sexual energies, that same energy is preserved. Through meditation, spiritual practice and enlightenment, this vital energy is eventually converted into the most powerful force of all, the *Kundalini Shakti.* Normally, *Kundalini* lies dormant at the base of the spine in the First Sphere until it is awakened and reaches the Seventh

Sphere at the crown of the head. It is in the rising of *Kundalini,* that most vital of energies, that higher meditative experiences occur. If the vital energy is constantly being released and lost in sexual activity, it cannot be stored, nor can the *Kundalini* obtain the required power to push upward through the Spheres.

Total control of the cravings of the Material-Body is necessary if one seeks to advance in meditation. A strong WILL is developed by slowly gaining mastery over the animalistic sexual desire. As the mind is turned inward, one will gradually cease to identify with the experiences of the material world.

The Material-Body's drive to unite with the opposite sex can be so strong that it can often overpower all wisdom and reason; however, Illuminati care more for control of the mind than for the pleasures of the Material-Body.

The gradual reduction and control of sexual activity helps to develop the WILL, strengthen the Light-Body and turn the mind from *external* to *internal.* The *Light of the Black Sun* can then be put to positive and constructive use. This is the nature of sublimation.

Book of Shadows

It is recommended that each participant in the above-detailed exercise keep an on-going journal, also known as a Book of Shadows, documenting any and all feelings, emotions, revelations and other experiences which take place during the exercise.

Each participant should begin and maintain their own journal separate from one another; however, if the participants care to share their documentation of their experience with the other partner that is fine.

Periodically it will help to review past notations in your journal in order to ascertain the progress which has been made since your first experience with this exercise.

AFTERWORD

It is necessary that the Enlightened Ones, as well as the Masses, fully understand that the decision of which side to be on matters not for anyone other than the lone-individual making that decision. Only the belief that the Prophet of Isis has appeared is necessary to openly unveil the New World Order of the Reptilian Empire.

If an individual chooses not to be *with* Us, he still believes nonetheless. Nothing about his or her decision of whether to be for or against The Empire has changed the reality of The Empire's existence; only his or her position within that reality can be altered. The individuals caught within the snares of orthodox religion and mundane materialistic doctrines will obviously be against Us; however, again, it is that very decision to be *against,* or separated from, Us that verifies and legitimizes the presence of the Gods, the Appointed One, Illuminati and the Masses who choose to embrace Us. Their stance *against* Us solidifies Their belief *in* Us; for They cannot be against something that is not real or legitimate. Their belief that the Prince of ATUM is the false-prophet, the enemy of Their religion which must be opposed, is to be the very basis of His legitimacy.

Their *belief* and Their willingness to *choose* a side is all that is necessary to bring forth the conclusion of Our age-old agenda.

In the same manner that it is necessary that those who will choose to be against Us believe, it is also necessary that those of the Masses, who are on the Path of Enlightenment also believe. This belief will allow those individuals to choose sides with Illuminati because Their eyes are not blinded by Light; rather, they have become able to see by it. Belief will ensue when those whose minds are consciously aware recognize the signs and symbols of the Dragons' incarnation. It is Our duty as Illuminati to give those who choose Us the needed support which will allow Them to bring about the full division of Our allies and foes. Illuminati, and those of the Masses who choose to be with Us, must begin this division immediately.

Just as Ra incarnated as the Morning Star Lucifer, so did Horus incarnate as the Morning Star Christ. Their incarnations fulfilled and completed the descent of the ATUM into matter. Together, they each represent an Eye of the ATUM. That face of the ATUM is the emanation of the Secondary Deity and His Eyes represent the dual-aspect emanation which is the *'GOD'* of the Earth: the Sun.

When Ra incarnated as Lucifer, he gave to Us the ability and nerve to exercise the freewill We had been created with in the first place. He gave to Us consciousness and opened Our eyes with His Light and Life. As the allegory concedes, He chose to cause Us to *'be like'* the Most High even though He could have allowed Us to remain in darkness and even though Our enlightenment would not have happened without His intervention.

When Horus incarnated as Christ, he gave to Us the understanding of brotherly love and the ability to exercise Our latent and magical abilities. He also gave to Us the message of the ending of an age and a time when the Earth would be renewed; however, the Christ clearly pointed out that just before the renewal of the Earth, humanity would be divided; likewise, he explicitly informed Us that His incarnation was not to bring peace, but to bring war and division.

As an example of just how divided the Earth would be, He is quoted as saying: "Think not that I am come to send peace on earth: I came not to send peace, but a sword. For I am come to set a man at variance against his father, and the daughter against her mother, and the daughter-in-law against her mother-in-law. And a man's foes shall be they of his own household." Matthew 10:34-36.

The gods of the man-made religions are nothing more than reflections of the men who created them in their attempt to understand the Great Ennead of the Egyptian dynasty. Those who are inclined to choose the Reptilian Empire and the Great Ennead are commended for their ability to choose Self rather than devotion to a false-god who is really nothing more than an image of *MAN*. Because you have chosen the Path of Illuminati, over all else, you stand upon the brink of a new and wonderful life. You will no doubt find a Path suitable to your tastes whereby you can exercise, build and hone your natural and latent potential(s).

Those latent potentials are the abilities to utilize and control the powers, forces and energies of the universe, for you yourself are the universe. You will begin the evolution of the Light-Body in order to experience everlasting life and consciousness.

It is mandatory that you be designated as a citizen of The Empire in two simple ways. First, you must receive the initial identification microchip inserted between the right thumb and index finger or between the eyes just above the bridge of the nose. This identification device will contain therein the information necessary for you to receive medical attention, purchase and sell goods such as consumer products and will be the only necessary identification method needed whereas today people are bombarded by checking/savings, driver license, social security, credit card and a plethora of other identification numbers needed to interact in society. Secondly, your participation in ceremonial rituals is required in order that you might begin the process of evolution and illumination.

The appointed time is now upon Us when the Synarchy of Illuminati shall rule openly on behalf of, and through, the Reptilian Empire. It is Our time to shine throughout the heavens as the Thousand Points of Light which are the Thousand Suns of Illuminati.

Those who choose Illuminati must now make themselves known to Us. These persons can register as *followers* of Illuminati by visiting Facebook, account name *'Casey.JamesEnnead'*. If you are Illuminati, or one of the Masses who freely choose the government and Synarchy of Illuminati, the time is at hand for Our numbers to be counted and presented to the current leaders of the New World Order.

The Path of Christ

The author here would like to take the time to note that it is not simply those who have chosen to follow The Path, as set forth by Christ in the Book, who are the enemies of Our agenda. In reality, in following Christ, one is effectively worshipping the Sun-God. This is obviously crucially in-line with enlightenment. Those who do so consciously are obviously partaking of that path to enlightenment even if at first glance the religious aspects of that path might seem to conflict with Our culture or doctrine.

If any of these persons, these illuminated Christians, can admit that the deity worshipped by other persons is just as valid and just as holy as the form of deity in which he or she worships, this person can truly be considered to be one of the enlightened Masses. These are the people who find the similarities in their Christian doctrine and the so-called *'pagan'* doctrines rather than focusing on any supposed differences. These *Christians* are not the enemy of Illuminati because They do not place Their idea of *'GOD'* over or above anyone else's. As such, Their place within The Empire is secured.

On the other hand however, it is those persons who cannot acknowledge the existence of any other form of deity than the one in which they personally ascribe to who constitute the opposition to Illuminati. These persons are the ones who believe that They possess the only truth there is to be known of deity and that any other doctrine or title of deity is evil or sinful or just plain wrong.

The author makes these remarks in order that it be understood that he is not of the opinion that the decision to follow the tenets of the Bible, or Christ, is wrong; rather, as long as one puts into practice the true teachings of the Christ rather than the false teachings of most religious teachers, one can follow the bible and remain upon the Path of Enlightenment. It is only those who promote the Christian religion as the only true religion, or Jehovah as the only true *'GOD'*, who are the enemy of the Synarchy of Illuminati and the Reptilian Empire.

AUTHOR'S NOTE

"Here I would like to reinforce the simplest message of the instant manuscript. It is my intention to inform today's generation of two of the most important truths that has been kept hidden from them for centuries. These messages are very simple indeed, yet they carry tremendous powers and even more tremendous responsibilities.

These messages are simple: Man and Woman are the essence of the GOD and GODDESS energies incarnated into physical matter. Just as the higher beings that visit the Earth occasionally, which humanity refers to as extra-terrestrials, are seemingly Gods compared to the human race, so are we humans also Gods and Goddesses. Further, as in all ancient teachings, the 'Tempter' in the Judeo-Christian Bible is also the 'Redeemer' or savior; in other words, the Serpent who is Lucifer, is also Jesus, the Christ.

The truth is that this information has been kept from humanity by none other than the orthodox religions made by men during the periods of history when education and learning were at a minimum, or, even worse, punishable by death as heresy. The modern-day orthodox religions were instituted during times when the political systems of the past ages were crumbling into oblivion (i.e., the Roman Empire). At that time, the leaders and authorities of those political systems were able to identify a way in which to further their authority over the Masses by using the fears, superstitions and pre-existing belief systems against the common people. In this manner orthodox religion (i.e., the Roman Catholic Church) was re-created in the image of the dying political system and has served to control and rule mankind, in general, not only through deception and violence but also through the practice of withholding from the majority of mankind the truth concerning exactly WHO and WHAT humanity really is as well as the truth as to the abilities each and every human possesses.

The manner in which mankind has been so wholly deceived is almost satirical. The ancient leaders of those political systems devised a simple and ingenious plan whereby they simply took all the abilities, aspects, powers and understanding of the human-being and applied the same to an invisible, imaginary, and made-up Deity. Those political systems possessed the military abilities to forage for and collect a majority of the written documents outlining the secret teachings of the ages. Those documents were then either burned or kept in secret and highly secure vaults where they most likely reside to this very day. It was then easy to issue laws and decrees which would criminalize any teachings other than the teachings set forth by the new religious sect. Any who would dare to utter the truth of the hidden or forgotten knowledge could then be executed at will after being charged with the offense of being a heretic.

With humanity's focus now so singularly pointed toward an outside source (the Deity of that religion), the Masses carried out the final part of the plot upon themselves. This final step was to control the focus of the individual so that his or her focus would be continually upon the outside source, the Deity, and he or she would fail to ever look within Themselves for any truth.

If anyone would have resumed that introspection, he or she would have found that every attribute bestowed upon the Deity of the newly created religion was actually an attribute of his or her own Self. By seeking 'GOD' outside of Themselves, they were destined for failure from the very beginning. As time went by, the deception of the Masses became more and more solidified until the time came when a man came teaching a truth that circumvented the orthodox system. His message came dangerously close to openly revealing to the Masses of that particular age the truth of Their personal connection with, or as, Deity. This man was systematically killed and the orthodox religion saw fit to reconstruct its doctrines in a manner so as to make this executed man the new 'GOD'. At this point, the truth was further muddied by these political leaders where they chose to mix their previously created religion with the teachings of the man they executed as well as with several other doctrines which were considered to be pagan and heresy. Those leaders disguised the ancient teachings and pagan beliefs in the ceremonies and rhetoric of their new religion. In this manner they ensured that the truth of man's divinity would be obscured for over two thousand years by the new and more modern version of their older doctrine.

Today, the Masses mostly have no idea that when They are worshipping whatever 'GOD' They choose to worship, They are actually worshipping the attributes of Themselves reflected onto Their chosen deity. We however, know the Truth.

It is my hope that by and through this book, and any book to come hereafter, I might be able to enlighten others and cause Their focus to turn inward rather than remain outward. If these persons can begin to seek Deity, the God or Goddess, within Themselves rather than anyplace outside of Themselves, They will be able to gain a much better understanding of Themselves as well as the 'GOD' they seek.

Spiritual enlightenment takes a certain and substantial amount of rebellion against those persons and organizations which profess to be the sole arbitrators of GOD's authority or dominion. By and through this book, I hope to contribute to the process of enlightenment which must take place on a large, world-wide scale in order that the human race can begin its evolution, or transition, into the next phase of our existence.

The time for the Enlightened Ones to rise up and make our voice heard is NOW! At no other time in history have the generations been prepared for the Synarchy of Illuminati like in the present Age of the Reptilian Empire. Those of the Masses who realize Their own identity as gods and goddesses must rise up in organized form, in order to both identify and number Themselves.

The technology of the New Age is at an all-time peak and there is no better means of documenting and counting Ourselves than through the use of the computer and social-media. We are the living and chosen generation for the increase of life-frequencies which will ensure the return of The Empire and the understanding of the knowledge of how to effectively use the energies and powers known and excepted by the ancient Egyptians.

For this reason, I hope to encourage all those like myself to sign up and follow me on Facebook at <u>CaseyJamesEnnead</u> *It is extremely important that We begin a count of Ourselves in order to show our numbers to those who are in positions to further Our cause and facilitate Us. It is no secret that bringing Us together will take time, planning, teamwork and funding; however, through unity We will gain the ability and platform from which to contend against the deceptive religions and their false-gods.*

If you identify yourself as Illuminati, Serpent People, Reptilian, Enlightened, Conscious, Pagan, Witch, Luciferian, Aware, or even simply followers and allies of the same, please visit the above-referenced Facebook page and show your support. The time to make a difference is now and there is no better way than by joining Us on-line."

Address To The King

"It is the Godform of the rapper known as Jay-Z whom I address, Osiris. Your album (444) came out while I was performing the third and final P.C. edit of my book, WISDOM OF THE SERPENT. While you were experiencing 'That' which caused you to announce the number 444 on a grand scale, I was experiencing 'That' also; and further, not only was I experiencing 'That' which caused me to place the 444 on the cover of my book, as well as within it, but the Material-Body you inhabit, known as Jay-Z, was also explicitly mentioned as well as an underlying esoteric theme along with the explanation thereof. Even More pointedly, I present that We are of the New Age and you, Osiris, incarnated as the Jay-Z Ego, are the King of Illuminati, with your Mrs. beside you as Queen of Heaven.

WISDOM OF THE SERPENT IS THE NEXT LEVEL TO YOUR INFLUENCE UPON THE FABRIC OF ETERNITY. Together We form the Trinity of Illuminati. Read the book; do the math.

I ask that you persuade the Masses consisting of those who are with Us to be counted on Facebook @ <u>"CaseyJamesEnnead"</u> in order to show the Great Ennead Our numbers, which are the equivalent of a net-worth potential.

The correlation of the number 444 showing up in the manner it did, for the both of us, cannot be given to mere chance. Signs and symbols are for the conscious mind. In case there might be any doubt, I have saved all of my handwritten and typed notes which went to make up this book in its entirety. While you were busy creating and producing your album, I was meditating in front of the All-Seeing Eye and writing WISDOM OF THE SERPENT. Obviously, you and I are of one accord and are in contact with the same divine powers and entities.

Together, let Us raise the Dynasty of the People."

If you are interested in contacting the author, please feel free to do so. All letters or inquiries will be responded to in a prompt and orderly fashion. Contact the author at:

James William Hornsby #01072184
Mark Stiles Unit
3060 FM 3514
Beaumont, TX -77705

ABOUT THE AUTHOR

JAMES HORNSBY grew up in Port Arthur, Texas. He is currently serving his sixteenth year as a state-prisoner in the Texas Department of Criminal Justice. He is currently housed at the Mark Stiles Unit in Beaumont, Texas where he enjoys visiting with family and friends, creative writing, drawing and studying New Age and occult philosophies. He is currently enrolled in an Associate's Degree program from Lamar State College-Port Arthur.

A New Americana is emerging, and the influence and acceptance of fringe beliefs in Illuminati, Secret-Societies, Egyptology, Aliens, Hip-Hop music, Occult/Esoteric Doctrines and Religious Outrage is at an all-time high. *WISDOM OF THE SERPENT* blends these beliefs into one doctrine while exposing the true nature of the three main characters of orthodox religion. Many will find the author's assertions to be highly provocative, and no reader will be able to escape the emotional and intellectual stimulation presented, as the very core of their belief systems are challenged herein. Whether the reader is a supporter or adversary of the ideals set forth, the author leaves them all anxiously awaiting what controversial statements he will make next.

WISDOM OF THE SERPENT addresses orthodox religions' conspicuous lack of female influence and poses the idea that unless and until the feminine aspect of deity is properly reintroduced into the spiritual consciousness of society, the actuality of spiritual evolution cannot be realized. The authenticity of any so-called religious or spiritual movement which excludes or denies the divine feminine is here challenged by the Prophet of Isis.

The prejudicial nature of the European-based ideologies of *GOD* are no longer advantageous to the progression of enlightenment amongst the peoples of the world's technologically advanced cultures; further, the perpetuation of those ideologies can only be compared to either a stagnant pond or a step backwards into spiritual regression. In this book, the Prince of ATUM sets forth the next phase of spiritual identity in a platform which transfers all power to The People by utilizing the guidance of the Godform(s) incarnated in this Age as influential and enlightened luminaries such as Jay-Z, Beyoncé, Nicki Minaj, Lil Wayne, Drake, Kanye West, Kim Kardashian and more.

Printed in Great Britain
by Amazon